5

FIVE
LITTLE
QUESTIONS

that REVEAL the LIFE GOD DESIGNED for YOU

GUIDED MEDITATION JOURNAL

DANNAH GRESH

FIVE
LITTLE
QUESTIONS

that REVEAL the LIFE GOD DESIGNED for YOU

GUIDED MEDITATION JOURNAL

THOMAS NELSON
Since 1798

NASHVILLE DALLAS MEXICO CITY RIO DE JANEIRO BEIJING

Published in Nashville, Tennessee, by Thomas Nelson. Thomas Nelson is a trademark of Thomas Nelson, Inc.

Thomas Nelson, Inc. titles may be purchased in bulk for educational, business, fund-raising, or sales promotional use. For information, please e-mail SpecialMarkets@ThomasNelson.com.

Five Little Questions
that Reveal the Life God Designed for You
Guided Meditation Journal

ISBN-10: 1-4185-2834-X
ISBN-13: 978-1-4185-2834-8

Printed in the United States of America
07 08 09 10 RRD 9 8 7 6 5 4 3 2 1

CONTENTS

CONTENTS

A Note from the Author

Hello, friend:

Do you ever feel like a rat on a spinning wheel trying to hold it all together but dreadfully aware that you're getting nowhere fast?

You're not alone. Not even close.

Fifty percent of women say they'd like to transcend their busy schedules to figure out the meaning and purpose to life. Mind if I help you get out of that 50 percent? Welcome to *Five Little Questions that Reveal the Life God Designed for You: Guided Meditation Journal*!

I love books that change my life. The ones that change my life usually require me to roll up my sleeves and do a little work. This Bible study is my personal invitation to do just that, but I'm going to be working right alongside you. I want to help you dig into God's Word to find the life God designed for you. I'll use excerpts from the companion book entitled *Five Little Questions that Reveal the Life God Designed for You*, brand new material that God has put on my heart, and guided journaling to respond to the *Five Little Questions*. The study will rely heavily on meditating on God's Word. It's an age-old discipline created by God Himself and poorly counterfeited recently by the new age movement. I'll introduce or re-introduce the discipline to you, and you'll find that it brings power to the words that you read, enabling them to change your life.

I'm so excited to take this journey with you. I just know that if you ask Him to, God will blow you away. Let's begin!

—Dannah Gresh

INTRODUCTION TO PART I

FIVE FEARS THAT STAKE US TO MEDIOCRE LIVES

I am confident that this Bible study has mighty power to reveal the specific life God designed for you, but not because *I* have insight into what God says about your life plan. Oh no! The power comes from the insight you will offer in your response to God. I've read so many books that requested meditation, rumination, stillness, and Spirit-drenched quietude, but for so long I never knew how. I want your meditation to be substantial, energizing, challenging, and fulfilling. And in case you've never tried this before or you're in need of refreshing your passion for meditation, I'd like to guide you.

I learned to meditate on God's Word about ten years ago from my friend and counselor Tippy Duncan, and it has revolutionized my prayer life. What is meditation? A pastor I know defines it as "what happens when studying a verse and praying collide." I like that. Great word picture. Within each study session from this point on, I'll make sure we dig into God's Word for some meaty knowledge about one specific verse. That's the studying part. We'll do that work together.

Then, I'll ask you to read that key verse and pray and listen for God to reveal something to you about it. If you've never done it, here's how to get there:

- First, read the verse and simply pray, "Dear God, please reveal to me the specific truth you have in this verse that's just for me. Help me to recognize your voice." I encourage you to do both out loud if you can. It squashes distractions and seems to yield better results.

The five little questions reveal
God's best life for you.

- Second, roll the verse around in your mind or on your tongue. Speak it. Think about it. Consider what your study has just revealed. Something might happen right away, or you may need to sit in silence. Just be still and "listen" with your heart. Some women report "seeing" a visual picture of interpretation. Others have words pop into their heads. You may feel emotions as God touches you with the truth of the verse. It could seem terribly subtle the first few times you try this. Don't be timid. Go with what pops into your head, as long as it is in agreement with Scripture. Don't stop until God really does give you something that's just for you.

  If I'm really stuck, sometimes I begin to doodle in my journal. I focus on the verse and just draw what it looks like to me. My journal is full of pictures of vines and eyes and thrones and crosses.

- Finally, simply receive it. Thank God. Praise Him. Commit to obey Him. Whatever the appropriate response is, express it either verbally or in writing. I like to write a journal entry about what I receive from the Lord during meditation. And sometimes, if it is really powerful and I don't want to forget it, I write it right in my Bible.

During the first half of this Bible study, a main goal is to become so comfortable with meditation that it feels natural and you're confident when you hear God's voice whispering to your spirit. You see, when we get to the second half, it'll be all out warfare with the enemy of your soul as you begin to get all-too-close to God's plan for your life. Hearing from the Lord with confidence will be critical to moving into the life God designed for you. So, in this first half not only will we be analyzing any fears that stake us to mediocre lives, but we'll be producing meditation muscle to use in the second half. Remember we'll be answering the five little questions that reveal the life God designed for you. They're very practical—cognitive, if you will. However, if you answer them solely by reasoning, you may miss God's fantastic plan. You've got to answer them in conjunction with an in-tune heart.

What *are* we waiting for? No need to roll up your sleeves just yet. Simply turn the page. Let's get you living the life God designed for you.

FEAR #1: THERE'S NO HOPE FOR ME

I pray also that the eyes of your heart may be enlightened in order that you may know the hope to which he has called you, the riches of his glorious inheritance.
—EPHESIANS 1:18

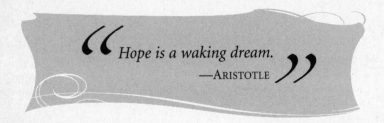

" *Hope is a waking dream.* **"**
—ARISTOTLE

I am so delighted that you have chosen to roll up your sleeves to do the serious work of discovering the life God designed for you. I'm here to work right beside you. What we are about to do is life altering. There's no turning back. Once you see a glimpse of the life God designed for you, you'll never be satisfied with anything less.

I have one word of caution. Don't do this halfway. Satan knows how much damage one woman living in a God-designed life can inflict upon his dominion. He'll stop at nothing to discourage and dissuade you. If you're only in halfway, you'll never survive. Commit to doing this all the way!

§ What are three expectations you have as you embark on this journey with me?

1. _____

2. _____

3. _____

Write a prayer of dedication as you begin this journey to find the life God designed for you.

_____

_____

_____

FROM FIVE LITTLE QUESTIONS...

Hope is born of suffering.

Our spirits rise up to grasp hope when the doctor says, "It's cancer."

We have little but hope to reach for when the World Trade Centers fall.

We eventually find our way to hope's door after Enron takes our life's savings.

It seems in the face of the worst of suffering, hope comes quickly. But where is the friendship between hope and suffering when that which causes suffering is mundane, normal, common? When it's just how it is? Where is the hope when we can't find the courage to get out of bed to work two more jobs for even one more day? To try one more time to pass that difficult class? To run at a breakneck pace for one more week? To juggle the demands of family and career? Or to reach out for a dream our friends and family don't believe in? Where is the hope when our spirits tell us our lives are drastically off course? Where is the hope in this suffering?

The Bible warns that you will not find the hope for freedom from a purposeless life in conventional wisdom, but that the great, exciting, blessed riches of God's purpose for your life are "hidden." (Ephesians 3:8, 9) That doesn't mean that you can't find your purpose. The Greek word *anaexichniaston*—

don't ask me to say that—is what ends up in our Bibles as "hidden." It meant "that which could not be traced by human footprints." So enter the rat race if you want, but I think you'll find that those human footprints won't lead you to the great, exciting, blessed riches of God's freedom for you. To find those you have to follow the sovereign footprints of God.

Incidentally, the footprints of God *have* been followed. Evidence of this is found in a reference to the Israelites as they journeyed from Egypt, their place of bondage, to freedom.

• Read Psalm 77:19 and paraphrase it below. What is specifically noted about God's footprints?

_____

_____

_____

_____

They didn't see them. The Israelites did not see the footprints of our Almighty God. Ah, but they followed them. And so must we, but how do we follow them if they are not visible to human eyes? That's one of our greatest challenges. How do we get out of this mediocre existence by following God's footprints? Certainly we can learn something from the Israelites who also wanted out of bondage to slavery—a very mediocre life.

• Read Exodus 13:17, 18. Again, God is leading the Israelites. This is when they are just beginning this journey, as are you and I.

Describe the route God chose for the Israelites to take out of mediocrity.

Why did he select this route?

_____

_____

_____

This passage of Scripture chronicles the Israelites' first steps to a life of purpose and freedom. The path they were asked to follow was rocky and difficult. Why? Because we so quickly build beautiful pictures of our places of bondage and God doesn't want to make it easy to go back. Take warning, this journey may not take you on the easiest path, but I promise some "milk and honey" at the end. Rest assured, God will take you on a path that disables you from turning back.

About one year after the Lord had called me to write my first book, we were feeling the financial tension. I was no longer working with my husband in our marketing firm, and it would be another year or two until my book was released. During this season the Lord was calling me to be a wife and a mom in a new way, and He was asking me to slow down and be undistracted so I could hear Him. I *knew* I wasn't supposed to go back to marketing, but my favorite client begged. She offered me twice the going hourly rate for market consultation. It was too much temptation. I took the work. I missed the adrenaline rush of a job well done, and I thought we needed the money. It is so easy to go back! Within just a few months, this relationship, which had been so precious to me for nearly ten years, ended very badly through a misunderstanding.

Why is the path sometimes difficult? So you can't do what I did and what the Israelites considered so very often. God doesn't want you to go back once you've begun this journey. Remember that and know that He's going to be working hard on your behalf.

• Read Exodus 14:19. Who had been traveling in front of Israel?

_____

Where did he go and why?

_____

_____

_____

_____

The angel of the Lord had been traveling in front of them. I believe this pattern is supported through Scripture. God leads. We follow. My sense is that He tore up the route from one side of the Red Sea to the others, opening wide the waters with His glory. Then, the way prepared, He turned back. In this rare instance, He withdraws from leading in order to jealously fight the enemy to protect His beloved Israel. Take comfort! If you can't sense Him in front of you, He may be behind you fighting off the enemy.

• Read Exodus 14:26–31. This is the passage that chronicles the exact moments, referred to in Psalm 77:19, which reads, "Your path led through the sea, your way through the mighty waters, though your footprints were not seen." What is going on in the physical realm when the Israelites were stepping over those footprints of God?

_____

_____

_____

_____

_____

Moses lifts his hands as God instructs and the sea opens up. Would you have been the first to walk between the walls of water? I certainly would not have. (My adventuresome husband might well have given it a thought, but even he may have cowered at the awesomeness of what was about to take place.) How their hearts must have pounded as they walked across that sea-bed! I can just imagine Moses standing there, his arms held high in the air as over two million families of clumsy Israelites craned their necks to see if their man was still standing.

Ephesians 1:18 reads "I pray also that the eyes of your heart may be enlightened in order that you may know the hope to which he has called you, the riches of his glorious inheritance." This path we're looking for in your life—it's something human eyes cannot see. You've got to look with the eyes of your heart. Eyes only God can supernaturally open. While there may be amazing things happening in the physical realm, keep looking with your heart.

Unfortunately, we live with such a powerful paradigm of the physical world that we can have a hard time shifting from our physical eyes to our spiritual hearts. We need God to open the eyes of our hearts. This seems to work best when we look right into the face of our fear that "there's no hope for me."

In what area of your life have you lost hope? Finances? Your ability to become a mother? The hopelessness of always being a bridesmaid, but never the bride? Where does your fear that hope is gone bed down in your life? Write about it here.

_____

_____

_____

_____

_____

_____

Now, look at it square in the eyes and . . . are you ready for this . . . let go! Tell God He can have it. Dare to stop grasping so tightly to the hopelessness of the physical world so you can begin to see what He is up to in the spiritual world.

MAKING IT WORK / MEDITATION

I pray also that the eyes of your heart may be enlightened in order that you may know the hope to which he has called you, the riches of his glorious inheritance.
—EPHESIANS 1:18

Your meditation assignment for this study session is Ephesians 1:18. Remember, simply read it. Then, ponder it thoroughly as you pray. Savor this. Do it slowly and don't miss anything God might have to say to you. Finally, write a response to God or record what he's revealed to you right here in this book.

If at anytime you feel insecure in how to proceed with meditation, turn back to the introduction to this section on Page 1. Review my guidelines and ideas for meditation.

Whatever you do, don't skip this vital part of our journey together. It is the main tool that God will use to reveal the life He designed for you.

GUIDED MEDITATION SESSION 2

Read Along in Five Little Questions: Chapter 3

FEAR #2: NOTHING WILL EVER SATISFY ME

The Lord says, "All who are thirsty, come and drink ... Why work for something that doesn't really satisfy you? Listen closely to me, and you will eat what is good; your soul will enjoy the rich food that lasts.
—ISAIAH 55:1–2 NCV

> *One of the most important discoveries I have ever made is this truth: God is most glorified in me when I am most satisfied in him.*[1]
> —JOHN PIPER, AUTHOR OF *DESIRING GOD*

Too many Christian women are living lives that just happen to them. They aren't impassioned by or satisfied with their life. It lacks meaning and purpose. God didn't ever intend for you or I to live like that.

Are you satisfied with your life as it is? Do you feel passion for this day that you're living in right now? Or do you dread the work ahead?

On a scale of 1-10, rate your satisfaction level for your life?

Not Satisfied 1—2—3—4—5—6—7—8—9—10 Very Satisfied

If you haven't already, read Isaiah 55:1–2 on page 12. What a sensible passage. Why work for something that doesn't really satisfy? Why work a job just for a paycheck to pay your bills? Why attend a parents' association club meeting only to fill time? Why bake cookies for Bible school just because you were next on the phone list? Why work for something that doesn't satisfy? There has to be an underlying purpose to it all.

There is an underlying purpose to it all.

And when you find it, you'll drink deeply of refreshment for your soul that is good. Even some of the things that you now find mundane, you will be able to approach with an enthusiasm you didn't have before.

Is there something—or perhaps many things—in your life right now that you approach with dread rather than a sense of knowing you'll be satisfied?

_____

_____

_____

_____

_____

The root of our struggle for satisfaction is extremely deep. It's rarely about being stuck with doing the laundry, having to take an upcoming test, or even surviving a struggling marriage. These are the surface issues we have to dive beneath to get to the heart of the issue. That's where more meditation comes into play.

One of my personal rules for powerful meditation is to be fueled with the wisdom of great Bible scholars. Otherwise, I end up just interpreting Scripture based on how I feel and, perhaps, what I want it to say. When I first realized that I was never satisfied by anything in my chaotic life, I took on the task of some research. I knew that I needed to stop making changes based on how I felt. Those changes were never permanent. I'd soon start to feel bad about something new. I wanted the changes to stick!

My research led me to a document about the Bible called *The Westminster Confession of Faith*. (Stick with me here for a quick historic detour. It's important.) In the mid-1600s, the battled and bruised Church of England desired to make right the zealous and often murderous misrepresentations of Christianity. (Translated: They were way off course just like you and I can be.) The Westminster Assembly was established to study and thoroughly interpret the Bible so that Christians could live according to God's Word, not the whims of the culture. The biblical scholars appointed by Parliament began the task of writing the *Westminster Confession of Faith* in 1643. It took five years to write it. Forty-two years later, it was critically analyzed by the Church of Scotland and adopted. Eighty-one years after it was originally completed, it was again scrutinized by the Philadelphia Synod of the American Presbyterian Churches. Though a few minor paragraphs were deleted, it stood out once again as a solid statement of beliefs for the Christian. My point is that it's been scrutinized carefully. It is best known for its widely supported statement of the purpose of man. Perhaps you've heard these words.

See if you can fill in the blanks to this famous statement from the Westminster Confession. (Yes, this is a test. And, just so you know going into it, I failed the first time I took it.)

"The chief end of a man is to_____ and to _____"

I was able to recite that "the chief end of man is to glorify God," but I came up short with the rest. Little did I know that this was a revelation concerning how very much in bondage I was. I'd embraced a half-truth about who I was in relation to God. Half-truth is not truth at all, and it was enslaving me to a half-hearted duty to God. Everything I did—from parenting to publishing our community paper—was done out of a sense of duty.

The full statement from the Westminster Confession reads, "The chief end of man is to glorify God and to *enjoy* Him forever." When I read that, something in my spirit cried out. This fast-paced life of duty wasn't my chief end after all. Some of the wisest students of the Bible just told my spirit that it was supposed to be finding joy in life.

I wasn't.

I was more certain than ever that this was not how it was meant to be. And that my fear that I could never be satisfied was simply not true.

It's not true for you either.

- Read Ecclesiastes 3:13 and write a summary of it here.

_____

_____

_____

_____

_____

_____

_____

God's end result of provision in your life—food and clothes and shelter—*is* satisfaction. Are you experiencing that? One of my early fears in seeking satisfaction for myself—and one that many women face—is that others would suffer. My husband. My children. My coworkers. My team of volunteers at church. I wanted them to be happy.

- Read Exodus 18:23. Then, hold that verse in your head while I give you some context for it.

Exodus 18:23 takes us back to Israel. Moses has long since been used as a tool to part the Red Sea. He's now going about everyday life and a big part of his job is to judge between any disputing parties. His father-in-law, Jethro, comes to visit and sees the terrible chaos of one person being the end-all solution to over two million families' problems. (Don't judge. It's easy to see when the numbers are that high. But is it possible you do this on a smaller scale?)

Jethro offers him a better idea. Appoint capable men who fear God to sit as judges. Only the truly difficult cases will be passed on to Moses.

What does Exodus 18:23 say the end result is when we find the God-designed way of doing things?

_____

_____

_____

_____

_____

_____

Jethro's promise rings true for you and I. He says, " . . . you will be able to stand the strain, and *all these people will go home satisfied!*" Building holy boundaries in your life so you can enjoy it does not rip apart everyone around you. They may have a challenge in making the change with you, but ultimately they are satisfied, too!

List the ten most important people in your life.

_____

_____

_____

_____

_____

_____

_____

_____

_____

_____

Do you have any fear that they'll suffer if you pursue the life God designed for you?   ____Yes ____ No

If you answered "yes," I need you to know that this is an unholy and untruthful fear. First of all, "God does not give us a spirit of fear but of power and of love and a sound mind" (2 Timothy 1:7, NKJV). If you are sensing any fear, it is not from God. Second, if you live the life God designed for you, everyone around you will be satisfied. Scripture promises it and so do I. I'm not saying the adjustment won't be a challenge, but the end result will be something everyone loves.

Just as Jethro was able to see the situation more clearly than Moses, so God sees your situation more clearly than you do. Talk to Him. Ask Him how to find satisfaction.

MAKING IT WORK / MEDITATION

The Lord says, "All you who are thirsty, come and drink . . . Why work for something that doesn't really satisfy you? Listen closely to me, and you will eat what is good; your soul will enjoy the rich food that satisfies."
—ISAIAH 55:1–2 NCV

Let's give meditation another try. Now, if you didn't feel you got much last time, don't give up. It does take some time. There are times when I meditate and don't feel like I get a lot. But let me give you a dose of enthusiasm by showing you what can happen when we meditate.

Thomas Chisholm had a pretty ordinary job. He was an insurance salesman in Warsaw, Indiana. I can only imagine he had a personality with some drive since he was a salesman. Often those of us who are driven find it hardest to slow down for meditation. I can imagine that he had an awfully long to-do list. What salesman doesn't?

One morning, Chisholm stopped on his way to work. He sat by Winona Lake and meditated on the goodness of God. That day, as he watched the sun rise, he wrote the words to "Great Is Thy Faithfulness." What a wonderful hymn of our faith that has become.

Biblical meditation causes a powerful interpretation of God's Word for you . . . and sometimes for the world around you.

Your second meditation assignment is Isaiah 55:1–2 (NCV).

_____

_____

_____

_____

_____

GUIDED MEDITATION SESSION 3
Read Along in Five Little Questions: Chapter 4

FEAR #3: THERE'S NO TIME TO FIX IT

At the right time [kairos], *I heard your prayers ... I tell you
that the "right time"* [kairos] *is now.*
—2 CORINTHIANS 6:2 NCV

> *You'll never miss your calling if you are
> seeking the heart of God. Just be with Him.
> He'll send you out.*"[1]
> —BETH MOORE, AUTHOR AND BIBLE TEACHER

An African church story tells of a pious man who came to church each Sunday. A man who couldn't seem to live a godly life, he would weep and zealously pray for God to "remove the cobwebs from his life." And yet, as the rest of the week wore on there was no effort to connect to God. No attempt to hear from God about what he could do to change his life. One week, another church member who'd become exasperated by this man's constant crying for God to remove the cobwebs from his life pointedly added, "And, Lord, while you are at it, please kill the spider!"

How like that man we can be. I once was like him, thinking myself such a devotee of Christ but all week being far too busy to invite Him into the chaos. Things never got better. I was cleaning the cobwebs out of my life each Sunday, but the spider of busy-ness still reigned.

It's fruitless to try and find the incredible freedom of living in your life's purpose without the vital step of claiming alone time with just you and the God of the universe. Author Beth Moore says, "You will never miss your calling if you are seeking the heart of God. Just be with Him. He'll send you out." She supports this with Mark 3:14, which says "Jesus chose twelve and called them apostles. He wanted them to *be with Him*, and he wanted to send them . . ."(NCV).

• Look up Mark 1:17. How does this passage support Beth's thought?

It literally says, "Come, follow me, and *I will make you* fishers of men . . ." Don't let the end of the verse distract you from the overwhelming message of the four words I italicized. Do you see it? Come, follow me. I will make you . . . leaders of nations . . . facilitators of book clubs who speak for the Christian worldview . . . mothers who raise children after God's own heart . . . managers who exemplify Christian excellence in the workplace . . . party planners who love Him . . . authors . . . artists . . . teachers . . . musicians . . . wives of passion . . . purpose-filled women! He does the making and the sending! We just get to spend time with Him.

What does your heart beat to become? Really! Dream with me, now. If the spider of being busy could be squashed, who would you be and what would you do?

_____

_____

_____

_____

_____

_____

You can be that . . . if it's a big dream, that is. God has not called you to be ordinary! He has called you to an extraordinary life. That requires an extraordinary investment of your time, but not in the way we naturally invest it.

Many years ago, I was called through a book by author Becky Tirabassi to spend an hour a day with God. It revolutionized my life. I became almost immediately changed. My life was purposeful and peaceful. I began to accomplish world-changing things, if just within my own community.

When did you most recently feel the power of prayer unleashed in your life?

_____

_____

_____

_____

_____

May I confess to you that in the last six months I began to question my call to pray for one hour a day? I was losing my discipline. When everyone else is watching *American Idol*, I really can't. (Though I am a shameless "*24*" addict!) I have to make choices that others don't to carve an hour a day out of my life. One too many people challenged me that this practice was legalistic. So, I just stopped.

Have you ever been so overwhelmed with prayer—either the responsibility of it or a lack of results or an inability to connect—that you just wanted to quit or did?

_____

_____

_____

_____

_____

During my time of frustration, I said only one prayer each day. It went like this. "God pursue me."

He did.

First, He let me feel all-too-much of what I felt years ago before I started being with Him. Isolated. Over-busy. Confused. Over-busy. Grouchy. Did I mention over-busy?

Then, he decided to bring Becky Tirabassi to my hometown through some of my closest friends. Her message: get with God for one hour a day. I've begun again and I'm delighted to say the change was once again nearly immediate. Can I just say it simply?

He makes me good. He makes my life good.

I just have to stay close to Him.

Have you ever been pursued by God to pray?

_____

_____

Why do you think He chases after us and invites us to "pray without ceasing?"

_____

_____

_____

_____

• Read 1 Corinthians 9:24-27. How are you supposed to run in this race of life?

_____

_____

_____

FIVE LITTLE QUESTIONS STUDY GUIDE

According to this passage, what kind of training or discipline will it take to win?

_____

_____

_____

_____

_____

At the time that the apostle Paul wrote this, the Corinthians hosted Olympic-style games every three years. He refers to these games in this passage. Certainly he was fully aware that these games revolved around wrestling or fighting, which is referenced when he says, "I do not fight like a man beating the air." Did you know that these fights were to the death? One was crowned. One was buried. There was no middle ground! How like our lives I believe this to be. We are either running to win a great crown and thankfully the Lord has many to present to the disciplined runners, or we are dying a slow death to a mundane existence buried under our busy chaos. Both take much time. Only one ends with a prize. Think you don't have time? Think again!

FROM FIVE LITTLE QUESTIONS...

Speaking of time, the word *kairos* shows up in the Bible as time. It has two basic meanings. One is a "particular or appointed time." The other is "the right or opportune time."

All of the following verses use the Greek word "*kairos*." Match each to what you believe is the use of the word in these verses.

A-"particular or appointed time"

B-"the right time"

"Repent, then, and turn to God, so that your sins may be wiped out, that times [*kairos*] of refreshing may come from the Lord" (Acts 3:19).

"And pray in the Spirit on all occasions [*kairos*] with all kinds of prayers and requests. With this in mind, be alert and always keep on praying" (Ephesians 6:18).

"[You] . . . who through faith are shielded by God's power until the coming of the salvation that is ready to be revealed in the last time [*kairos*]" (1 Peter 1:5).

"Blessed is the one who reads the words of this prophecy, and blessed are those who hear it and take to heart what is written in it, because the time [*kairos*] is near" (Revelation 1:3).

The first two use the "right or opportune time." The later two use the "particular or appointed time."

Meditate for just a moment and ask the Lord how these two definitions link beautifully together. Write out your conclusion.

_____

_____

_____

_____

_____

_____

_____

The "right or opportune" time seems to generally act as a call for you and I to commune with God . . . not when we feel like it, not when we're desperate, not when it's convenient, but now! I really sense that it is our job to invest our time [kairos] now into being expectant for *the* time [kairos] of His return. That's the link.

Above all, we are called to prepare our hearts and souls to be in eternal communion with God. We will live in His presence! And, we must look expectantly to that. It's more important than the dishes, your upcoming deadlines, signing the kids up for yet another after-school activity, and anything else on your to do list. We've got to take time for God.

The irony of it is this. We must have expediency in our hearts to slow down. We must understand how vital it is to just be with Him now, so we can be ready to be with Him later.

Why not invest some right now?

MAKING IT WORK / MEDITATION

> *At the right time* [kairos], *I heard your prayers . . .*
> *I tell you that the "right time"* [kairos] *is now.*
> —2 CORINTHIANS 6:2 NCV

Take it from this nighthawk who is writing to you at 11:28 PM and going strong—sometimes mornings are not the very best part of your day. I try to begin my day in prayer, but then I set aside a time that's more productive for me to sink into the presence of God. As you meditate on 2 Corinthians 6:2, don't ask God *if* you should start to schedule daily time to be with Him. Rather, ask Him *when* it should be. Where should it be? Will you need a CD player for worship music? A candle for the quieting of your heart? (A lock on the door to keep the kids and four-footed critters out?) How much of your day should you schedule with Him?

Your third meditation assignment is 2 Corinthians 6:2 (NCV).

GUIDED MEDITATION SESSION 4
Read Along in Five Little Questions: Chapter 5

FEAR #4: MY PAST DISQUALIFIES ME

*Praise be to the God and Father of our Lord Jesus Christ. God is
the Father who is full of mercy and all comfort. He comforts us
every time we have trouble, so when others have trouble, we can
comfort them with the same comfort God gives us.*
—2 Corinthians 1:3–4 NCV

"What is denied cannot be healed.[1]
—Brennan Manning, *The Rabbi's Heartbeat*"

Are you living under the weight of the fear that your past may disqualify
you? How common a fear that is. Satan once cleverly sidelined me with
this fear. I was absolutely certain that no girl who called herself a
Christian should fall into sin the way I had. And certainly, the secrets
my heart held disqualified me from doing anything of significance for
God. How heavy the weight of it can be.

Experiencing God, a Bible study by Henry Blackaby, is based on the
miraculous, God-filled, adventurous life of Moses. He was a murderer.
That fact was not lost on this sinner as I pursued the practical
application of the study and sought my purpose by hearing God's voice.
Blackaby writes, "When God gets ready for you to take a new step or
direction in His activity, it will always be in sequence with what He
already has been doing in your life. He builds character in an orderly
fashion with a divine purpose in mind." Those two sentences
revolutionized my thinking about my past. God was saying, "Dannah, I

want all of you. Not just the 'good stuff'. What I'm planning is in sequence with where you've already been. Stop being a fugitive. Come out of hiding."

What area of your life do you hide?

_____

_____

_____

_____

Do you find that you sideline yourself from
certain things at church because you feel
hypocritical if you'd serve in that way?   ____Yes ____ No

If so, what things?

_____

_____

_____

_____

Do you ever find serving God to be unfulfilling?
It's just something you do because
your name was next on the phone
list to bake brownies for Bible school
or your turn has come up in nursery?   ____Yes ____ No

Explain your answer.

_____

_____

_____

_____

Psalm 50 gives me a fresh dose of this truth when I need a reminder of how small my works are in an attempt to glorify God.

- Read Psalm 50:9–12. What does God say about our routine acts of service and our works of obligation?

_____

_____

_____

_____

According to these verses, how *can* we glorify God?

_____

_____

_____

_____

Talk about getting dissed. God is saying, "Get this. I don't really need you. There's nothing you have that I don't have more of. If I were starving, I'd not even bother to ask you for food!" He's basically saying that our works are just petty attempts to bring Him glory. How then can we glorify Him? He explains: *Call me in times of trouble. I will save you, and you will honor me.* The Hebrew word for *honor* means glorify. He is glorified in our rescue. The very thing we'd like to hide is the part of us that speaks of His power.

I tire of the country-club Christianity that I see so often in churches today. It would seem that we are simply gathering for social purposes because we vote the same way, have kids in the same schools, and like the same kind of worship or Bible teaching. Who'd have ever guessed we were actually pitiful sinners in need of a Savior? We're that picture-perfect! It's time we allowed the world to know our rescue stories so that we can really begin to glorify Him.

§   What has Christ rescued you from?

_____

_____

_____

_____

_____

2 Corinthians 1:3, 4 is a treasured passage. Summarize it below.

_____

_____

_____

_____

What gift do we have to give to others if we've allowed God to truly heal our most broken places?

_____

_____

_____

_____

31

I can *see* sexual pain on teenage girls. I cannot tell you how it works. It is one of those things I don't see with my physical eyes, but with spiritual eyes. Sometimes the Lord allows me to approach them, but often I'm called to pray. No matter what, I'm ready to share my story with them out of a place of wholeness and healing. I do not have this same gift when it comes to eating disorders. I can't say that I frequently sense the emotional or spiritual struggles of a teen boy. As a teen girl, I knew the extreme pain of sexual sin. And, I found God's comfort. It's only natural to pass it on.

FROM FIVE LITTLE QUESTIONS...

Is there a place of sin in your past that still hurts to talk about? A divorce? An abortion? Alcoholism? Debt?

Perhaps it's not your own sin, but the sin of someone close to you that has veiled your hope to glorify God in wounds still seeping with unforgiveness. Your husband's battle with pornography? Your dad's incestuous touches? The judgment of a congregation?

It doesn't have to be a sin at all, but it could be deep pain that cripples you in your quest to pursue God's purpose for your life. Is this the past that haunts you? A broken family? Cancer? Infertility? The failure of a business? The loss of a child? Or, even sadder, that your sheltered past is relatively irrelevant to where people are today? Oh, how sad when a clean testimony feels like no testimony at all.

It is time to stop living under the weight of the fear that your past disqualifies you. It's time to begin living under the weight of glory. Now that God is using me, I've got a greater responsibility to embrace the truth of His covenant consequences, as will you if you move forward in freedom to pursue the life that God has designed for you. It's a much easier weight to carry. It is a joy to carry it. Why don't you join me?

MAKING IT WORK / MEDITATION

"Praise be to the God and Father of our Lord Jesus Christ. God is the Father who is full of mercy and all comfort. He comforts us every time we have trouble, so when others have trouble, we can comfort them with the same comfort God gives us."
—2 CORINTHIANS 1:3–4 NCV

Got a "past"? Give it to God for His glory. Hiding it is really only a quest to glorify yourself. In hiding your past, you hide your sin and make yourself look better. You glorify yourself. You also hide God's rescue—the very place of His glory—and you make our faith a routine and steady observance rather than a life-changing powerful reservoir of healing. Release it. How can you know if you need to release it? Well, put your life up into the light of 2 Corinthians 1:3–4. Whom have you comforted with the comfort God has given to you?

GUIDED MEDITATION SESSION 5
Read Along in Five Little Questions: Chapter 6

FEAR #5: I'M GOING TO FAIL

We have freedom now, because Christ made us free. So stand strong.
Do not change and go back into the slavery of the law.
—GALATIANS 5:1 NCV

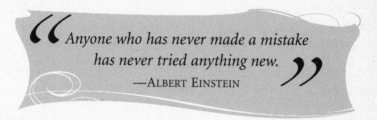

"Anyone who has never made a mistake
has never tried anything new."
—ALBERT EINSTEIN

Nearly every single new thing God invites me to facilitate for Him comes packaged with the fear of failure. I hear an argument in my heart for each calling:

* When God calls me to help repair a marriage that's falling apart: "You *know* your own family will suffer. Remember the brokenness of busy-ness you once knew?"

* When God calls me to confess my temptations and sins with a new friend: "You *know* you'll never be able to trust her. Remember when your friendship with _____ fell apart and all the stuff she used against you?"

* When God calls me to build a piggery in Africa to fund abstinence education: "You *know* you won't be able to finish it. Remember how _____ tried to help in that other country and made a fool of herself?"

35

- When God calls me to submit to a decision my husband is making: "You *know* he's not going to protect you, and you'll rise up in anger again."

- When God calls me to support my husband in founding a new Christian high school: "You *know* there'll never be enough money for it. Remember the bondage of your business debt?"

- When God calls me to do something that a few of my friends and family members can understand: "You *know* you'll look like a fool."

The greatest fear I face from time to time is that the sins I've overcome will return to overcome me. These are fears about sexual sins, financial debt, and struggle to control my tongue.

Do the sins of your past ever rise up in your thoughts to convince you you'll just fail again?

_____

_____

_____

_____

What outright sins have you fallen for? Perhaps you'll write about the same sin you were hiding in the last guided meditation?

_____

_____

_____

_____

If you were to honestly evaluate any socially acceptable sins that you've fallen for—overeating, overworking, boastfulness, etc—what would they be?

_____

_____

_____

_____

_____

Again, being very honest, what intellectual sins have you fallen prey to but can now see more clearly—humanism, pride of educational status, evolutionary compromise, etc.

_____

_____

_____

_____

_____

What financial failures as a result of greed or disobedience to God have you ever experienced, if any?

_____

_____

_____

_____

_____

What failures do you fear right now?

_____

_____

_____

_____

_____

It can be so easy to fall into sins from the past. A singer/songwriter once wrote a song called "Clumsy" and sang about "reaching out for that same old piece of forbidden fruit." I can identify. It seems to be the same thing over and over again. Perhaps not to the same degree, but old habits die hard. What do we do with the fear that we're going to fail? If you're looking for me to comfort you with the fact that you won't go back to the same old stuff, don't wait too long. I don't think that's how it works.

Summarize Galatians 5:1.

_____

_____

_____

_____

What is God calling for us to be aware of?

_____

_____

_____

He's calling us to be aware—very aware—that we could lose ground. We could go right back into the things that once enslaved us.

FROM FIVE LITTLE QUESTIONS...

Interestingly enough, the Greek word contained in our warning to not "go back into slavery" gives us a vivid picture of how we most often lose our freedom. The wording is a common word for being trapped as if by a snare.

A snare isn't your typical steel foothold trap, which looks painful and nasty with its iron teeth. No, the snare is far more subtle looking. It's a simple piece of steel cable, which forms a loop. It appears non-threatening, if it is even noticed at all. When an animal walks through the snare, it walks calmly. It just keeps walking through it, feeling nothing. Soon it may feel a little tension, but it just plods on. As the animal feels greater tension, it pulls harder and presses forward. Soon its own force of movement has enslaved it to the snare. It doesn't realize that if only it had backed out earlier, it could have gotten away. By the time it recognizes that it's stuck, it's too late. The capture is subtle and is empowered by the animal's own actions.

What a vibrant picture. It is our own actions . . . our own decisions to move forward . . . our own quest to keep up with the Joneses that get us into such a place of bondage.

I realize it is commonly accepted to call problems people have with drinking an "addiction to alcohol," but I do wonder if maybe it wouldn't be better if we called it a sin of drunkenness. If I have an addiction, it's workaholism. I could say it's hereditary. I could say at times in my life I seemed powerless against it. I could say I've made some very bad, risk-filled choices that have harmed my family because of it. I could call it an addiction to work, but it would be better if I called it sin. I've worked hard to avoid this subtle trap of the enemy because when I walk into it, I become less productive and more consumed with my plans than with God's design for my life.

A few years ago, I noticed myself walking into the snare of work addiction once again. I was placing my own force of actions into a carefully designed trap of the enemy. I was becoming consumed by my love of work. I realized that I was missing my son's sophomore year of high school. I also realized that I didn't know which room Lexi's dance class was in because I hadn't been there early enough to watch her practice. (She delights in being watched.) Though I've found boundaries to protect me and my family, the sin of busy-ness was consuming me.

I had to rein myself in.

§ Ever experience something similar? Write about a time when a snare you'd overcome had become a real threat to your spiritual vibrancy once again?

_____

_____

_____

_____

_____

_____

Now, please understand that I'm not saying that you should blindly give in because it is hopeless to overcome your sin nature. I don't believe that for a second. I've come so very far. But when I have fallen, it has been because I naively believed I was beyond it. I'm never beyond anything without the grace of Jesus Christ.

As you begin to live in the life God designed for you, Satan will do everything he can to see you fail. He'll tempt you with things you'd long ago gotten over. He doesn't play fair. Be wise. Acknowledge that, aside from God's grace, you are toast!

MAKING IT WORK / MEDITATION

We have freedom now, because Christ made us free. So stand strong.
Do not change and go back into the slavery of the law.
—GALATIANS 5:1 NCV

As you meditate on Galatians 5:1, let the Holy Spirit guide you in which direction you should go. He may want you to confess that you have been ensnared. He may want you to ponder the fact that you've become self-sufficient and believe yourself to be beyond your old temptations. He may want you to be soothed by the fact that a recent fall from grace is completely covered in His blood. The direction He could take you with this verse is broader still than even these suggestions. This verse is extremely powerful. Meditate until you sense with certainty where you are to go with it.

_____

_____

_____

_____

_____

GUIDED MEDITATION SESSION 6

Read Along in Five Little Questions: Chapters 7-11

FINDING THE FREEDOM TO LIVE THE LIFE GOD DESIGNED FOR YOU

All have sinned and fall short of the glory of God, and are justified freely by His grace through the redemption that came by Christ Jesus.
—ROMANS 3:23, 24

"*Sin . . . blocks contact between the natural and spiritual worlds. Sin introduces a kind of static interference in communication with God and as a result shuts us off from the very resources we need to combat it.*[1]
—PHILIP YANCEY"

Traveling too fast can be hazardous. Four years ago, I went with my family to Kruger National Park in South Africa. It's one of the world's largest game preserves. Lions, giraffes, cheetahs, rhinos, and more awaited our discovery in the wild African bush.

We entered the park, which was nothing more than vast, dry jungle land and dirt roads. A hand-painted sign read, "Warning: Do not under any circumstances exit your vehicle. Animals are wild!" A flurry of smaller signs had the names of lodges within the park painted along with arrows. We found ours and headed off on our little dirt road. Up and down dips in the dust. Through curves and turns. Miles later, we were still going. I guess Bob got impatient because he soon began driving faster and the kids literally loved banging their heads on the roof of our SUV as we bounded along. Until, on one bump in the road the entire vehicle was airborne. We heard a funny sound.

A few yards later we were stranded. No 9-1-1. No traffic passing by.

No air-conditioning. Just the 95-degree African sun beating down on us. I've never felt less safe, wondering if at any time a lion would jump out of the bush and into our windows to have a little snack.

After much prayer, the Lord sent along a phone service provider who kindly took us to our lodge. We found out the next day that, in fact, a lion had been spotted on that road the day we were stranded. And, just a week before, two tourists had decided to get out of their vehicle and one was, in fact, lunch for the lion they were hoping to photograph.

No, going fast is never a good idea. That's why we've started our journey toward the *Five Little Questions* with the five common fears women face. We're getting there slowly and thoroughly to assure success.

Which of the five fears is one that you've struggled most with in your life?

1. There's no hope for me.
2. Nothing will ever satisfy me.
3. There's no time to fix it.
4. My past disqualifies me.
5. I'm going to fail.

How have you struggled with this fear?

_____

_____

_____

_____

Write a prayer to God asking Him to completely deliver you from this fear as you move toward answering the *Five Little Questions*.

_____

_____

_____

_____

_____

Now, I know that I just said we shouldn't go fast, but I've been down this road before. We're at a place where we can go fast. We're going to cover a lot of territory quickly in this guided journaling session. I want to strongly advise that you read through chapters 7-11 in the companion book, *Five Little Questions That Reveal the Life God Designed for You*, before you begin this session.

FROM FIVE LITTLE QUESTIONS...

You cannot move forward in your pursuit of a God-designed life until you have identified what specifically shackles you to a life of mediocrity. You must be free to move forward.

What is freedom? It's defined as "the absence of restraint in choice or action" or "not being unduly hampered or frustrated." In the context of our quest together, the definition must be linked to freedom as it pertains to the life God designed for you. So, add to the definition clearly expressing the link between freedom and your purpose.

What is freedom? Fill in the blanks.

"The absence of restraint in choice or action _____"
OR
"Not being unduly hampered or frustrated _____"

What specific things do you see restraining you from your pursuit of the life God designed for you?

_____

_____

_____

_____

_____

Anything that restrains us from God's best is sin. Sin is what causes us to lack freedom.

Read the following passages and summarize what they say sin does to us.

John 8:34

_____

_____

_____

_____

_____

Hebrews 12:1

_____

_____

_____

_____

_____

I believe to truly see what restrains us from the pursuit of God and/or the pursuit of the purpose God has called us to, we must look carefully at the concept of sin.

Write a definition for sin below. Don't think hard about it. I want your first response.

_____

_____

_____

_____

_____

I think that, in general, the definition of sin that most Christians have in their heads is woefully incomplete. Perhaps yours is not, but let's explore things thoroughly. In our psychology-saturated world, it is quite understandable that we would be confused. Mark R. McMinn writes about our discomfort with the terminology of sin:

> "This is not just a mainstream psychology problem; it has affected Christian psychology as well. Philip Monroe, a faculty member at Biblical Theological Seminary, recently noted that only 43 of the 1,143 articles published in *Journal of Psychology and Theology* and *Journal of Psychology and Christianity* have been related to sin, and only four of those are related to the effects or treatment of sinful patterns. I wonder if we lost the language of sin because the language of psychology took its place."

You and I are going to claim some of that back, my friend. We're going to talk about sin, politically incorrect as it might be. To do so, we're going to go back to the original languages of the Bible—Hebrew and Greek. They are not only complex, but they were terribly wrapped into and dependent upon cultural meaning. I think that to mature in our biblical literacy, we must not only look at reliable translations of the Bible, but also search through what deeper meaning may be missed if we don't look at the original languages. Ironically, freedom is found in the definition of sin. We can only understand this if we roll up our sleeves to do a little language study.

The main Old Testament root word for sin is *chata* or *hatta*. It was an archer's term, which meant "to miss the mark." Now, if you were a skilled Hebrew marksman, what would you consider the mark of a target? The bull's-eye! You wouldn't want to settle for anything less. That's the intended purpose of your arrow. So this Hebrew word for sin means "to miss the bull's-eye."

GOD's BEST

Murder

God, as our designer, has designed a best life for you and for me. I want you to get this diagram into your head. We, at all times, need to be aiming for "the mark." *Anything* that distracts us from that is missing the mark. It's sin.

My perception of sin used to be that it was a beating stick. I could just imagine God pointing His finger at me in judgment and shouting, "You blew it! What were you thinking?" The rules of church made me believe that freedom wasn't really possible. The problem is we're looking at freedom backward. We think it's about pursuing our own desires. It's really about pursuing the life God designed. Sin restrains us in our choices and actions. It robs us of our freedom to pursue God. And that can be eternally dangerous!

Romans 3:23, 24 is a familiar passage. It reads, "All have sinned and fall short of the glory of God, and are justified freely by His grace through the redemption that came by Christ

Jesus." The New Testament, written in Greek, continues with the heart of the Old Testament's word for sin, *hatta*. But the Greek word, *hamartano*, expands the definition. It means "to miss the mark and so not share in the prize."

There's a reward.

This is the picture of discipline that God has now given to me. It is God stretching His arms toward me to pull me back into a safe place. I can just hear Him saying, "Oh, you've missed it. You missed it, Dannah! Don't you know what I had I store for you? Oh, try again! Try again!"

How does an understanding of this Hebrew word change your definition of sin as you wrote it a short while ago?

_____

_____

_____

_____

_____

Let me offer a concise definition for practical purposes. Nothing theological or grandiose. Simply this. *Anything* that restrains us from pursuing God's best for us is sin. *Anything*.

Our incomplete definition easily leads us to believe that murder or immodesty is sin.

But what about these seemingly innocuous things?

- Taking a job at the local university for the purpose of getting a tuition discount when you know you're called to invest full-time in the prayer mission of your community.
- Agreeing to bake cookies for Bible school when you can't bake worth a hoot, are over-scheduled and desperately need to invest more time into your marriage?

- Coaching your son's youth soccer team even though God's been speaking to you about cutting back on your social services so you can spend more time with Him since it's been months since you had any significant prayer time?
- Getting hooked on *American Idol, Lost, 24* and six other television shows, resulting in a tired body in the morning so you forfeit prayer time?
- Taking a job because it will pay the bills when you've been called to something that pays less but is a clear call from God?

Aren't these sins? Aren't they things that distract us from God's best for us—from His bull's-eye?

Given these examples, what is currently something that is restraining you from pursuing God's best in your life?

_____

_____

_____

_____

_____

Let's go back to our study of 1 Corinthians 9:24–27 from a few sessions ago. You are running a race to win a prize. There is a reward for the discipline it will require for you to live the life God designed for you. God says so outright in 1 Corinthians, and He marks it subtly in His definition of sin within the New Testament.

Look back at your notes from 1 Corinthians 9:24–27 on (Page 23). Remembering that there is no middle ground, what is the alternative to receiving the prized crown? Read the following passages and summarize what they say that confirms this fact.

Romans 6:23

_____

_____

_____

_____

Ephesians 2:1, 4, 5

_____

_____

_____

_____

Ephesians 5:14

_____

_____

_____

_____

I think God's salvation is about our eternal life, but I believe it is also about abundant life now on this earth. Malcolm Smith, author of *The Lost Secret of the New Covenant*, has forever changed my perception of death. He explains that God stated a factual truth to Adam and Eve about the tree of knowledge of good and evil when He said, "The day you eat of it you shall surely die!" Did they in fact die that day? Smith writes:

> "The problem with defining death is that those who are in the state of death are doing the defining and are convinced that they are alive! From their perspective, they are alive now and

death is what happens at the end of physical life; but the Bible plainly says that outside of Christ, they are not alive now. This is the world of the walking dead who do not live but exist."

God has such a grand reward for your life. I don't know what it is, but I know that it exists. He speaks of it throughout His word. Don't you want the prize of a life lived for Him? Or do you really want to hold on to a graveyard of a life?

MAKING IT WORK / MEDITATION

All have sinned and fall short of the glory of God, and are justified freely by His grace through the redemption that came by Christ Jesus.
—ROMANS 3:23, 24

Record the results of your meditation here.

_____

_____

_____

_____

_____

_____

_____

_____

INTRODUCTION TO PART 2
The Five Little Questions

You're doing it. You're investing the hard work of training to receive the prize. You've made it halfway through and you've set the stage to hear from God. Let's ask Him to reveal the life He's designed for you.

It's time to answer the *Five Little Questions*. Remember, we're going to use your practiced skill of meditation to do this. Otherwise, you'll just end up looking with your physical eyes. To see the spiritual realm, you must look with spiritual eyes. I hope you're beginning to see how fruitful meditation can be. It's so much more of a two-way conversation than many of our traditional models of prayer.

YOUR M.A.P.

As you answer the *Five Little Questions*, I'm going to help you build your own personal M.A.P. (That stands for "My Action Plan.") This will be a two-page plan or map to pursue the life God designed for you. You'll find it on the following double-page spread. After each guided journaling session, you'll come back to this spread to fill in what you've discovered about yourself and God's plan for you. So, grab a Post-it® note or bookmark and stick it in here so you can easily find this for the duration of our study.

At the end of each chapter, you'll find that I've expanded each section of this M.A.P so that you can think through things thoroughly before you fill it in on the comprehensive M.A.P. with condensed notes.

Oh, I'm getting butterflies! This is exciting!

What are we waiting for? Let's answer the first question.

MY ACTION PLAN
TO THE LIFE GOD DESIGNED FOR ME

*Welcome to your M.A.P. Those initials stand for My Action Plan.
As you use God's Word and quiet meditation to answer each of the
five key questions in this section, you'll fill out a new part of the
M.A.P. By the time we get to the last chapter, you'll have a concise
plan that will let you know exactly how to move
toward living in the life God designed for you.
Mark this page. You'll come back to it at the
end of each of the next five chapters. Don't
write in any section of these two pages until I
invite you to do so.*

Adornment
of Charis

Heart of the Mark

GOD's
BEST

the Ring
of Grace

THE RING OF GRACE

Do I Need A Fresh Infusion of Grace?

I entered into the ring of grace on

(date) _____ in (place) _____.

I received a significant fresh infusion of grace on

(date) _____ in (place) _____.

I commit to re-represent myself to God regularly
by taking holy communion. I choose from this day
forth that, no matter how it is presented to me, I will
make it an act of holy confession and intimacy with God. Specifically, some
goals I have established for myself include: _____

_____.

THE ADORNMENT OF CHARIS

Am I Working In Agreement With My Created Personality Type?

My personality type is _____.

I work best in an environment that is _____.

I need to make the following changes in my current work environment, home,
and volunteer projects to be able to work according to my personality strengths:

1 •_____   2 •_____

3 •_____   4 •_____

What's My Supernatural Ability?

My spiritual gifts include _____, _____, and _____.

I commit to dialogue with God about these and other gifts and to pursue those He confirms as gifts. This means I will avoid taking on ministry roles where I am working outside of my gifting.

◯ THE HEART OF THE MARK

Am I Enjoying God?

I enjoy God most in these ways, and I will seek to pursue Him through:

1 •_____ 2 •_____
3 •_____ 4 •_____

Am I Glorious?

In order to reflect God's radiance, I understand that I must rest in it. I commit to spend _____ minutes a day with God in Bible study and prayer from this day forward. I will schedule my time with God and write it right into my planner or calendar.

My God-Designed Life.

Now that you have a tip sheet, write a brief description of what your God-designed life looks like. Include any changes you need to make in your current life as well as any big dreams God wants you to pursue. In signing below, you commit to pursue what is outlined on these pages for the next six months.

_____

_____

_____

_____

Signed _____ Date _____

Accountability Agreement

Recognizing that I need to protect a life that is designed by God, I have shared my M.A.P. with _____. For the next six months, she is going to encourage me and pray for me DAILY as I pursue it.

Accountability Partner Signature _____ Date _____

GUIDED MEDITATION SESSION 7

Read Along in Five Little Questions: Chapter 12

QUESTION #1: DO I NEED A FRESH INFUSION OF GRACE?

Here I am! I stand at the door and knock. If you hear my voice and open the door, I will come in and eat with you, and you will eat with me."
—REVELATION 3:20 NCV

> *Quit keeping score altogether and surrender yourself with all your sinfulness to God who sees neither the score nor the scorekeeper but only His child redeemed by Christ.*
> —THOMAS MERTON

In some Arab countries you are likely to hear the saying, "Blood is thicker than milk." They're referring to the fact that a blood brother or sister is a closer relation than the brothers and sisters who drank the same mother's milk. They recognize how powerful and precious is a blood covenant.

Do we?

Our society offers not only less cultural meaning in understanding the holiness of our covenant with Jesus Christ, but it also approaches life informally and extends little value to honor and tradition. We just don't "get" covenant. I'm convinced that if we could grasp the holiness of our unbreakable, protective, sealed-in-blood relationship with Jesus Christ, we would never wander from it to grapple for the temporal satisfaction of sin.

But it seems to be wired into us to wander. Adam and Eve didn't take long to wander. In fact, Adam hadn't even named Eve before the Fall. The initial consequences were far more subtle than banishment from the beautiful Garden, toiling in labor and pain in childbirth. This initial consequence continues to greatly alter our ability to discern the life God designed for each of us.

Read Genesis 3:6–7. What is the immediate effect from taking the fruit?

_____

_____

_____

_____

_____

Meditate for a moment on what spiritual meaning this could possibly have. What are your conclusions?

_____

_____

_____

_____

Their immediate sensitivity to their nudity exposes a new level of awareness of the physical world. While I have to stop short at assuming that they were any less aware of the spiritual world, it can certainly be concluded that they suddenly had competition for their senses. Sensitivity to the spiritual realm would now be blocked by interference from the physical world.

There is nothing that disables your ability to discern the voice of

God more than sin. If you are looking for Him to provide a mystical answer to your quest for purpose, you can stop right now. If there is current sin in your life or sin in your past that you haven't allowed Him to heal, you'll never be released to your full potential in this life.

FROM FIVE LITTLE QUESTIONS...

Back to the mark . . . that specific pre-planned design of your life. Recall with me that the God-designed purpose of your life is found when you live in the dead center of the "bulls-eye." Anything less than hitting God' purpose for your life in every area—purity, joyfulness, financial stewardship, and even your vocational platform for your purpose—is sin. *Chatta.* That's right. Failing to find your life's purpose is sin.

There are three distinct parts of the mark, or bull's-eye. Each represents a vital part of our purpose. I believe you cannot even begin to live in the riches of God's purpose for your life until you first make a willful choice to accept Christ's gift of grace. In doing so, you build a "ring of grace" around your life. How do you do this? Surrender. In humility surrender your unbelievable neediness to Christ's forgiveness.

GOD'S BEST

the Ring of Grace

§ When did you first surrender to the grace of Jesus Christ? Be as specific as possible. Include the date, the place, and circumstances surrounding this powerful encounter with God.

How did this initial infusion of grace alter your life? What was different about you?

_____

_____

_____

_____

_____

Fill in the blanks of Revelation 3:20.

"Here I am! I stand at the door and _____. If you _____ ____ _____ and _____ ___ _____, I will _____ ____ and eat with you, and you will eat with me." (NCV)

It is really important to note that this verse was written to *believers* at the church in Laodicea who'd *already surrendered*. I can't count the number of times I've heard it misused as a call for the lost to surrender to Jesus for the first time. It is clearly not that.

What can you conclude that God was saying to them and is saying to us?

_____

_____

_____

_____

_____

Clearly, some of us wander far enough that we need to once again open our hearts to Christ or re-surrender. When we do this, God offers us a fresh infusion of His grace.

My life was drastically off-course twelve years ago. I was a believer who'd once surrendered, but I was living a self-designed life. And I was miserable. My re-surrender, which is documented in *Five Little Questions*, opened my ears up to hear God and my eyes up to see His hand at work.

I'm not so sure I *decided* to re-surrender as much as God pursued me. He showed up at the door to my heart and patiently knocked and knocked and knocked. He chased me down and loved me back into the center of His "ring of grace." Seems he's been doing that with humanity for a long time.

Read Genesis 3:21. What does God do for Adam and Eve after the original sin?

_____

_____

_____

_____

What happened to the animals whose skins God gave to the couple?

_____

_____

_____

This is the first recorded shedding of blood in Scripture and our first taste of covenant. Though this act is not classified as a covenant, there seems to be something going on in the spiritual realm. Follow my reasoning.

First of all, God certainly could have covered their nudity differently. Have you ever seen a fig leaf? They're huge! And, nicely shaped and colored. Eve may have looked smashing in her new skirt. What was wrong with that covering?

And, after all, He is *God*. He didn't really need anything to work with. He'd just created the world out of nothing. Couldn't He have whipped together a great ensemble for the newlyweds? He could have dressed Eve in an ensemble that would make Michael Kors look like a first-round loser from *Project Runway*. Instead, He chose to shed the blood of precious creation to cover Adam and Eve's nakedness. I think God was being intentional to require blood for this provision. Perhaps He was setting the stage for His blood covenants to come.

Covenant with God means that He is ever our defender. Always our provider. And because covenants are unbreakable, He will chase after us with an endless love.

And that always costs Him something.

I'm not sure we get that.

The Old Testament Arab world got it, as do many in the Arabic culture today. Because they get blood covenant. I offer a bit of a crash course on blood covenant in Chapter 12 of *Five Little Questions*, and I strongly encourage you to read through that prior to your meditation assignment today. But, let me offer one beautiful component of covenant for you to focus upon today.

Representation.

The ancient practice of covenanting has generally portrayed agreement between a lesser and a greater party. The greater party takes the lesser party into their protection. The greater party always required that there had to be a representative who acted on behalf of those in this agreed-upon ring of protection. This representative was a guarantor of the covenant and would act as a substitute or agent.

According to Hebrews 5:1, what role did the Old Testament high priest play in the covenant God made with Israel?

_____

_____

_____

_____

_____

Reading along in Hebrews 5:5, 10, who takes this role when the New Testament covenant replaces the original covenant with God's people?

_____

_____

_____

_____

Read Colossians 3:1–3. Who does God really see when He looks upon you?

_____

_____

_____

_____

Jesus, through His bloody death, sits as our representative at the throne of God. He was our representative when He died, and God issued our punishment to Him. Now when God looks upon us, He sees the Lamb.

Pastor Jonathan Wiebel, who travels with our teen ministry team, often talks of a beautiful word picture that helps me "get" it. In New Zealand, a land known for its wonderful wool, they practice something called "lambing." You see, when the baby lambs are born each year, many of them die in birth. And, many mother lambs or ewes also die giving birth. The farmers solemnly skin the dead baby lambs. Then, they drape the skin of the dead babies on top of the lambs who have no mothers. They take those blood- and fur-covered lambs to the mamas whose bleating reveals the loss of their own babies. But then, she smells the familiar scent of her baby and it's moving.

"Looks like my baby," says Jonathan when he shares this with teens. "Smells like my baby. And the mother receives the orphaned lamb as her own."

We can't really belong to God unless we are draped with the Lamb. God sees His Baby when He sees me. I can hardly comprehend it. Thomas Merton encourages us, "Quit keeping score altogether and surrender yourself with all your sinfulness to God, who sees neither the score nor the scorekeeper but only His child redeemed by Christ."

It seems many are far too content to receive one infusion of God's grace. That hasn't been enough for me. I need it again and again. I'm not suggesting I've ever lost what He first gave me when I was just a child. I just needed more of it.

As our high priest, Christ is not only representing us, but He also is constantly *re*-presenting us to His Father. It's what happens each time we partake of His blood and body in communion.

Going back to Revelation 3:20, what does God promise if we will open the door and let Him in?

_____

_____

_____

He will eat with us. This was no small thing. Jewish custom held that eating together was a great honor and an intentional extension of friendship. (Just imagine Jesus extending friendship to you!) Bible scholars also link this to the holy act of communion, which was intended to be a holy act surrounded by an intimate feast, as opposed to a quick passing of a cracker.

What I'm trying to get to is this. The practice of Old Testament re-covenanting through animal sacrifice was a constant process of re-presenting ourselves to God through the high priest. This is replaced by Holy Communion which, I believe, is meant to serve as a re-presenting of ourselves to God for a fresh infusion of grace. Perhaps, if we took it more seriously and handled it with greater holiness, we'd not veer so far off course to places where we are spiritually and emotionally depleted by sin in our lives.

Clearly when Jesus said, "This do in remembrance of me," He was calling us to come back for more grace again and again. He knew we'd never tire of it nor have enough.

He knew we'd be ensnared.

And, he'd stand knocking at the door to our hearts pursuing us yet again.

He knew you'd struggle for years in pain from that abortion. Or that you'd struggle to overcome lying. He knew you'd run into financial problems because of your problems with greed and lack of discipline. He knew you'd bear the burden of a prayerless life. He knew. And, He invites you to come back again and again to be re-presented to God for a fresh infusion of Grace.

This is where your quest for purpose begins. Not with your skills, talents and dreams, but with His grace. You'll never get to a God-designed life by any other route.

§ Have you ever received a fresh infusion of grace from God? Write about it.

_____

_____

_____

_____

_____

MAKING IT WORK / MEDITATION

Here I am! I stand at the door and knock. If you hear my voice and open the door, I will come in and eat with you, and you will eat with me.
—REVELATION 3:20 NCV

Now, for your meditation! The next few chapters' meditation assignments will be far more specific than they were in the first half of this study. They will help you answer the *Five Little Questions*. When you find the answers to the questions, you'll uncover a M.A.P. to the life God designed for you.

THE RING OF GRACE
Do I Need A Fresh Infusion of Grace?

Through this meditation, I want you to seek to answer the question, "Do I need a fresh infusion of grace?" Think about Jesus standing at the door and knocking at your heart . . . today. What's keeping you from opening the door? Has He been fully invited into your life? Does He have access to all of your life? Is there an area of sin in your life from which you've not healed? Is there any area of sin which is unconfessed or unyielded to Him? Do you need a fresh infusion of grace?

Your meditation assignment is Revelation 3:20 (NCV).

Now, turn to Page 54 and fill in the blanks in the first section of your M.A.P. under *"Ring of Grace: Do I Need A Fresh Infusion of Grace?"*

GUIDED MEDITATION SESSION 8

Read Along in Five Little Questions: Chapter 13

QUESTION #2: AM I WORKING IN AGREEMENT WITH MY CREATED PERSONALITY?

Train a child in the way he should go and when he is old he will not turn from it.
—Proverbs 22:6

" *When God made you, He put in your heart strengths, capabilities, potential skills, passions, drives and motivations. He designed you with a certain way of being. As a result, you feel fulfilled when you are acting according to your design—and frustrated when you don't.*[1]
—Dr. Charles F. Boyd "

A walk with Stormie, my labradoodle.

A bubble bath.

A quiet day of writing.

Time alone with God.

Preparing to teach a roomful of teenage girls God's truth about sex.

Nesting in my home by organizing and decorating.

These things fill me up. But don't ask me to do the laundry (again), to attend a staff meeting, to spend the day running errands or making phone calls. These drain me. I enjoy them as much as having a cavity filled.

What are your fillers? List at least five.

1. _____

2. _____

3. _____

4. _____

5. _____

What are your drainers? List as least five.

1. _____

2. _____

3. _____

4. _____

5. _____

God created you to be just like that. The same God who made my husband to be energized by team meetings made me to loathe them. I spent a lot of years in high-powered team meetings wondering why I was always drained and even very sick with migraines, sinus headaches, and colds. I was working outside of my God-given personality. And my body was trying to get the message to my spirit.

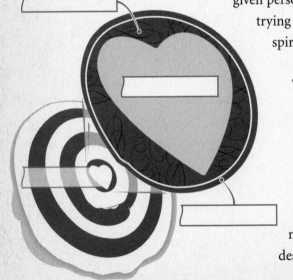

I'm a very visual learner. The fact that God has given us a very visual picture of sin is so good for me. And I truly believe that this picture houses three vital components to the bull's-eye that help us to create a map to the life God designed for you.

Look at the unlabeled diagram on the previous page and fill in the part, the Ring of Grace, we examined in the last chapter.

The five little questions help us to evaluate how successfully we're targeting the bull's-eye in each part of the mark. It will be good for you to memorize them because as you live in the life God designed for you, you'll need to make frequent adjustments to stay on target. The questions help you to evaluate yourself.

What question do you use to determine if you are staying in the Ring of Grace?

Do __ Need A _____ _____ of _____?

FROM FIVE LITTLE QUESTIONS...

Adornment of Charis

GOD'S BEST

the Ring of Grace

Getting into the Ring of Grace is just the first part of hitting the mark. Another vital part is what I call "the Adornment of *Charis*." *Charis* is the Greek word for grace. It literally means "gift." It also means favor, benefit, and blessing. A very significant part of God's grace is discovering the unique way He's going to favor your life with a gift to demonstrate His power. This is His Adornment of *Charis*. It's the part of you that's not like anyone else. It's the specific way God designed you to be fulfilled.

If you are feeling frustrated in life, it could be because you are working outside of your special personality strengths and capabilities.

Let's see if we can find them.

Fill in the blanks for Proverbs 22:6.

"_____ a child in the way _____ should go, and when he is _____ he will not _____ _____ _____."

Notice that the verse doesn't just say to train a child in *the* way, but the way *he* should go. What could this mean?

FROM FIVE LITTLE QUESTIONS...

Proverbs 22:6 encourages us to "Train a child in the way he should go." It is heavy-laden with treasure for us whether we are mothers or not. The first word, *train*, is *hanak*, an archer's term like the word for sin, *chatta*. This word was used specifically to describe a soldier training with his bow. The bows these ancient Hebrew marksmen trained with were not the gadgetry high-tech kind you and I see these days. Known as compound bows, modern bows can be adjusted to allow hunters of different sizes, strength, and skill to use them easily.

This was not so with the ancient "longbow." The bows these marksmen used were one simple piece of slightly curving wood. Each bow was uniquely different. Therefore, the hunter would need to adjust *himself* to the bow. He'd need to learn the bow's unique strengths and characteristics.

It gets even better. We're told to "train [*chanak*] a child in the way he should go." The Hebrew word for "the way he should go" is *derek*, which literally means "according to the bent." It refers to the unique inner design or direction of the child. The phrase, "the way he should go," doesn't speak of some prescribed path that every man, woman, and child should take. It's not talking about rules to live by. Rather, it is referring to a specific path that's just for this child. His or her unique design.

This verse isn't just for moms and dads. It's for you and me to apply to our own life. It's a hidden treasure in Scripture that invites you and I to figure out who you are. God wrote a personality into you before the creation of the world and when you work according to it, you'll find fulfillment. And you'll hit the bull's-eye.

The Marston inventory, commonly known as the DiSC inventory, is public domain and with it, I can get you somewhat pegged. It's not a thorough inventory, but if you've never taken time to test yourself this is vital. If you have, this is just for fun!

MARSTON'S PERSONALITY TEST

Number items in each set 1, 2, 3, or 4, with 4 being the statement that best describes you and 1 being the statement that least describes you.

A. _____ I often find myself telling people how I want things done.

B. _____ I'm animated and talkative and enjoy encouraging people to try a new way.

C. _____ I'm not that comfortable with being assertive. I'd rather follow others.

D. _____ I like to look at all the details and ask others if they've got them covered.

A. _____ I'm not that emotional in conflict. I just say it like I see it.

B. _____ I can be very emotional in conflict. People will know how I feel.

C.____ I am usually accommodating in conflict. I want everyone to be happy.

D.____ I am usually consistent and careful when conflict arises.

A.____ People might say that I am forceful with my opinions.

B.____ People would say that I am energetic and fun.

C.____ People would say that I am honest and quiet.

D.____ People would say that I'm tactful and careful.

A.____ I often feel that getting a job done is more important than other people's feelings.

B.____ I often don't care to work, but will talk things through with other people.

C.____ I'll help others get the job done, but I want to know it pleases them.

D.____ I want to get the job done right and will be slow and thorough.

A.____ People would say that I work quickly and on my own.

B.____ People would say that I work quickly but am distracted by people and things.

C.____ People would say that I work slowly but often stop to check my work with others.

D.____ People would say that I work slowly and on my own.

A.____ I prefer to be alone.

B.____ I am enthusiastic about being with people.

C.____ I am kind and compassionate around others.

D.____ I have very high standards.

A.____ People may perceive me as argumentative.

B.____ People might perceive me as fun and loving.

C.____ People may perceive me as patient.

D.____ People may perceive me as logical.

A.____ I like to take charge of group projects.

B.____ I am a visionary and often help groups get excited about a project.

C.____ I keep the peace and help a group stay unified when working on projects.

D.____ I am always concerned about keeping group projects organized and efficient.

A.____ I like new challenges if they are big enough.

B.____ I'm often impulsive, trying just about anything.

C.____ I'm encouraging to others when they try new things but may not join them.

D.____ I'm very unlikely to try something new.

A.____ I tend to be highly competitive.

B.____ I'm somewhat competitive, but mostly just like to be in the game.

C.____ I'm relaxed and rarely feel the need to win.

D.____ I like things to be done correctly and can be unglued if the rules aren't followed.

STEPS TO UNDERSTANDING YOUR RESULTS

1. First, add up the total of the numbers you placed beside each letter.

A.____ Total of all numbers placed beside A.

B.____ Total of all numbers placed beside B.

C.____ Total of all numbers placed beside C.

D.____ Total of all numbers placed beside D.

_____ Total of all A, B, C, and D should equal 100. If not, check your survey. You may have made an error or added up incorrectly.

2. Next, place a star or dot in the quadrant that reflects your strongest behavioral tendencies.

If A was your highest score, you are a Lion.
If B was your highest score, you are an Otter.
If C was your highest score, you are a Golden Retreiver.
If D was your highest score, you are a Beaver.

If you have two scores that are somewhat close, you may operate strongly in two areas. I do. Go ahead and reflect that on your score. You also may have three or four scores that are very, very close. That's called a balanced personality. Mark that on your diagram.

John Trent and Gary Smalley have come up with some tremendous portraits to help us remember our personality types and their character strengths. They write about them in their children's book entitled *The Treasure Tree*. They've given each letter a symbolic animal. I think this makes it so much easier to remember.

Whatever you are, note it on this chart by placing a star at the spot that best reflects where you are. For example, I'm a high A (Lion) with a lot of D (Beaver) in me. So I'd put my X on the line between Lion and Beaver to the far left since I don't have a lot of anything else in me.

My Behavior Style

Fast-paced Flexible

LION   OTTER

Task Oriented   People Oriented

BEAVER   GOLDEN RETRIEVER

Slow-paced Structured

LIONS—A (INTROVERTED AND FAST PACED)

If you score strongly in the A quadrant, consider yourself a lion. You're aggressive, assertive, like to lead, and are very task-oriented. You want to get the job done! You'll be a good decision maker, a direct leader, and will always be on the go with something new.

On the flip side, you might be a little impatient with people and tend to not be concerned with how they're feeling. You may be too controlling. You'll find details and routine work frustrating.

OTTERS—B (EXTROVERTED AND FAST PACED)

If you scored strongly in the B quadrant, you're an otter. You're the life of the party. You are friendly and enthusiastic and extremely flexible. You are strongly interested in influencing people and motivating them. You're a strong opinion leader and like to invite everyone to "the party."

Only problem is, you forget the details. So when we get to the party there may not be any snacks! You may even forget the goal and be sidetracked by something else. You'll need to develop the discipline to follow through with tasks and avoid work environments where you are in charge of all the details.

GOLDEN RETRIEVERS—C (EXTROVERTED AND SLOW PACED)

If you scored strongly in the C quadrant, think of yourself as a golden retriever. Just like man's best friend, you're loyal, supportive, and loving. You're very interested in how everyone feels and are great at helping people understand each other. You bring unity to the table. You'll love a position that enables you to be cooperative and supportive.

You may find that you have a hard time being assertive when you really need to be, but with some discipline this will come. Don't place yourself in a work environment in which you have to confront and manage a lot. It will stress you out. You'll also find that you don't like change and will be uncomfortable with a work environment that doesn't offer stability.

BEAVERS—D (INTROVERTED AND SLOW PACED)

Finally is our D quadrant. You are our beavers. You love to work. You are busy all the time making sure all the details are taken care of. You are detailed and cautious, so you'll get things done well. You'll enjoy work environments where you can be somewhat independent and organized.

You just might need to be flexible from time to time to be a good part of the group. Sometimes you'll be considered inflexible or rigid. You won't like to be in an environment where the pace is fast and always changing.

The question you want to answer is "Am I Working in Agreement with My Created Personality?" Without this step, I'd still be wondering why I was so frustrated with my marketing job. As an A/D (Lion/Beaver), I'm very task-oriented. I'm not people-oriented, which makes me somewhat of an introvert. As a result, my marketing job, which kept me in client meetings, staff brainstorming sessions, and sales events, drained me. I needed solitude so I could get tasks done. When we realized this, Bob, who was also my boss, put me in charge of marketing research and analysis of marketing surveys. And he moved my office into our house so I only came to the main office for necessary meetings. What a happy book-geek I was! This was a baby step closer to God's best for me, but I still wasn't entirely diving into the mark.

- Do you need more alone time or more time with people to fill you up?

- Do you need to work at a fast past or a slow one to feel fulfilled?

- What tasks or work environment in your life need to be modified for you to work within your God-given personality preferences?

- What baby steps can you take to realize those changes?

MAKING IT WORK / MEDITATION

Train a child in the way he should go, and when he is old,
he will not turn from it.
—PROVERBS 22:6

THE ADORNMENT OF CHARIS
Am I Working According To My Created Personality?

The second part of the mark is the Adornment of *Charis*. This is the part of the mark that is God's unique design in us. It makes us and our purpose entirely different from someone else's. There will be two questions we use to evaluate how you are hitting the bull's-eye in this part of the mark. The first is "Am I Working In Agreement With My Created Personality?" We often miss the mark because we don't understand our personality strengths. Do you understand your unique "bent" as it is called in Proverbs 22:6? This will help you to know in which environment you are best fulfilled. As you consider the verse, ask yourself if you're working in agreement with the personality God created in you.

Your meditation assignment in Proverbs 22:6.

_____

_____

_____

_____

_____

_____

_____

_____

_____

_____

_____

_____

_____

_____

_____

_____

Now, turn to page 54 and fill in the blanks in the first section of your M.A.P. under "Adornment of Charis."

GUIDED MEDITATION SESSION 9

Read Along in Five Little Questions: Chapter 14

QUESTION #3: WHAT IS MY SUPERNATURAL ABILITY?

But to each one of us grace has been given as Christ apportioned it.
This is why it says, "When he ascended on high, he led captives
in his train and gave gifts to men."
—EPHESIANS 4:7–8

> *Seventy-one percent of believers have heard of*
> *spiritual gifts. Only 31 percent of them can*
> *name one they believe they possess.*
> —BARNA RESEARCH ONLINE[1]

Singer/songwriter Rebecca St. James was asked what fills her up. (Remember that from our last session together?) She said, "I feel like one of my spiritual gifts is serving and helping, and I just enjoy that a lot." [2] She understands a very vital part of the adornment of *chara*. It's not just about whether you're introverted or extroverted or face-paced or slow-paced. It's not limited to the unique skills and personality strengths God has given to you. It's about your supernatural ability!

This is an exciting session, but before we proceed let's take the opportunity to build our memory of the *Five Little Questions* that will help you stay on the mark once we get you there.

Looking at the blank diagram, label both parts of the mark that we've explored or begun to explore.

What is the question to use to evaluate whether you are in the Ring of Grace?

Do I _____ A _____ _____ of _____?

What is the first question you can use to evaluate how you are doing at staying in the Adornment of *Charis*?

Am I _____ Within My _____ _____?

The second question that helps you evaluate if you are staying in the Adornment of Charis is "What's My Supernatural Ability?"

My friend, Lynn, thought she just had a great deal of women's intuition. She always seemed to know when someone her husband was hiring had a skeleton in the closet. They'd find out months or years down the road that she was right. Or she would have a terrible feeling in her gut when she thought about someone and would discover the next day that they'd been in an accident when she was having those feelings. Turns out she wasn't really intuitive. She'd been given a spiritual gift of discernment. That's the ability to sense things in the spiritual realm. It is her supernatural ability.

Do you believe you have a supernatural ability?

_____

_____

FROM FIVE LITTLE QUESTIONS...

I would like to encourage you to open up a dialogue with God about your supernatural gifting. I've found that His direction for me in this area comes over periods of years. So, the dialogue we begin today may just be a beginning or could be a continuation of one you've been having with God as you dig more deeply into gifts you have been aware of. But, please have a dialogue with God about your supernatural gifting. The entire body of Christ is depending on you to use it. It could have a globe-altering impact.

Fill in the blanks to Ephesians 4:7–8.
"But to _____ one of us _____ has been given as Christ apportioned it. This is why it says, 'When he ascended on high, he led captive in his train and gave _____ to men.'"

The word gifts, in this verse, refers to supernatural skills or abilities that are given to a believer when he or she surrenders to Christ.

Of those who have surrendered to Christ, who has been appointed to receive one of these gifts?
a. Only the spiritual elite
b. Those who were alive in Christ's time

c. Those who've been following Christ since their childhood

d. Each one

Each one of us is appointed to have a supernatural ability empowered by the Holy Spirit. Each one of us.

So, what's your supernatural ability?

SUPERNATURAL ABILITY INVENTORY

This is not a test and there is no scientific validity to it. I'm not even going to hide the names of the gifts I'm asking you to consider, which are the main gifts listed in the New Testament. (But if you read *Five Little Questions*, you know that God can supernaturally gift anything.) During this session, I simply want to encourage you to journal thoughts to God and explore passages that help you to discover or strengthen your understanding of spiritual gifts.

I really feel that spiritual gifts inventories most often measure our personalities and skills more than they measure our spiritual gifts. By nature of their source, these gifts often defy our natural skills and abilities. For example, I am an extreme introvert who at one time feared public speaking. I now operate strongly in a gift of teaching. Right before I speak somewhere, a strange stillness comes over me that I believe is the Spirit. I often take the stage with enough power to at least convince my audience that I'm an extrovert! They are often surprised when I tell them I'm a complete homebody who prefers a bubble bath and a good book to a Friday night bash. No test would have revealed this gift. God led me along gently encouraging me to unleash this gift. Prayer, circumstances, and opportunities have allowed it to present and mature as an anointed gift in my life, but I still often have to rely heavily on the Lord in prayer as I approach speaking engagements. Use my inventory here as just a jumping off point for a dialogue with God, but don't ever let any tool of man determine your spiritual gifts.

Let's begin your dialogue.

§ 1. **Circle your top three gifts from the inventory that follows.** It includes fourteen spiritual gifts, each of which is mentioned as a spiritual gift in Scripture. First, I want you to simply circle your top three. If you already know them, you can do that easily. If not, under each are some questions that will help you determine if this might be a gift you should begin to pray about. If you answer yes to several of the questions, it *may* be one of your top three.

ADMINISTRATION *(Romans 12:8, 1 Corinthians 12:28, Romans 16:1, 2, Ephesians 3:2)*

Do you enjoy setting goals, then leading a team toward achieving them?	Yes	No
Do you like to make decisions in times of crisis?	Yes	No
Are you able to see the "big picture" while managing the "small picture"?	Yes	No
Do you enjoy meetings, brainstorming, and finding people's passions?	Yes	No
Do you easily see how a project, a process, or an event could run more smoothly?	Yes	No
Are you comfortable confronting people that God places under you?	Yes	No
Would you prefer to delegate a task rather than do it yourself?	Yes	No
Do others recognize you as a leader and follow your ideas and plans?	Yes	No
Are you concerned about doing things in accordance with God's will?	Yes	No
Are you able to complete tasks that you begin?	Yes	No

EVANGELISM *(Ephesians 4:8; Ephesians 4:11; Acts 13:9–50; Acts 16:14)*

Do you often find yourself sharing God's love with random people?	Yes	No
Are you comfortable asking people about their relationship with God?	Yes	No
Do you enjoy conversations about God with people you've just met?	Yes	No
Do you tend to initiate conversations with people you don't know?	Yes	No
Are you often frustrated that other Christians aren't more evangelistic?	Yes	No
Are you often selected to train others to share the gospel?	Yes	No
Do you find yourself easily coming up with new ways to share the gospel?	Yes	No
Are you a bold and outgoing person when it comes to talking about God?	Yes	No
Do you tend to be the one in your church/small group to encourage outreach?	Yes	No
Are you always looking for an opportunity to share God's truth?	Yes	No

EXHORTATION *(Romans 12:8; Luke 7:37–50; John 12:18; 1 Timothy 5:1)*

Do others consider you to be a good listener?	Yes	No
Do you tend to have an optimistic outlook about people and their value?	Yes	No

Do you enjoy writing notes of encouragement or calling people in need?	Yes	No
Does God often seem to give you words of wisdom to share with people in need that you don't believe you'd have thought of on your own?	Yes	No
Are you able to confront people about sin without being offensive?	Yes	No
Are you able to see someone's sin without thinking the person is less valuable?	Yes	No
Do others tend to seek advice from you and follow it?	Yes	No
Are you able to motivate someone who's been discouraged or depressed?	Yes	No

GIVING *(Romans 12:8; Luke 3:11; I Peter 4:9; Luke 21:1–4)*

Do you tend to be disciplined with the resources God has given to you?	Yes	No
Do you hold your possessions loosely, enabling you to share them?	Yes	No
Are you disciplined in how you spend money?	Yes	No
When God gifts you with money, do you assume it is for His work?	Yes	No
Are you often willing to sacrifice to give more of your resources to needs you see?	Yes	No
Do people tend to trust you with knowledge of their personal financial needs?	Yes	No
Do you freely trust people to use the resources you share with them?	Yes	No

Does it make you happy to give money to help people or accomplish God's work?	Yes	No
Do others consider you to be responsible with money?	Yes	No
Do you give even when you have little to give?	Yes	No

MINISTRY/SERVING *(Galatians 5:13; Romans 12:7; 1 Corinthians 12:28; 1 Peter 4:11; I Peter 4:9; 2 Kings 17:9–16; Acts 9:36–41; Romans 16:1; Romans 16:12)*

Do you like to keep your schedule free so you are flexible to help others?	Yes	No
Do you tend to see others' needs easily?	Yes	No
Are you comfortable being involved in the personal crises of others?	Yes	No
Do you prefer low visibility when you serve?	Yes	No
Are you extremely loyal to leaders in your life?	Yes	No
Do you get pleasure in freeing others up from work that hinders them?	Yes	No
Do you like to keep your hands busy doing concrete acts of service?	Yes	No
Is it difficult for you to allow others to serve you?	Yes	No
Would you rather be in a support role than a leading role?	Yes	No
Do you prefer short, simple tasks to large, long-term projects?	Yes	No

MERCY *(Romans 12:8; Matthew 27:55–56; Matthew 5:7; Mark 5:19)*

Do you enjoy bearing the difficult burdens of those in need?	Yes	No

Do you find yourself able to love the unlovable?	Yes	No
Is it fulfilling for you to be strong for those who are weak?	Yes	No
Are you most fulfilled when you can help someone who could never pay you back for what you've done?	Yes	No
Do you often receive words of love, compassion, and sympathy from God for others?	Yes	No
Are you often inclined to help the aged or the ill or the poor?	Yes	No
Do others consider you to be tender and responsive?	Yes	No
Do you sometimes sense the needs of others before you are told of them?	Yes	No
Are you action-oriented; do you enjoy getting something done?	Yes	No
Do you love easily?	Yes	No

PASTOR/SHEPHERDING (*Ephesians 4:11; Mark 6:34; John 10:11, 12; Luke 15:14*)

Do you prefer being with people to being alone?	Yes	No
Do you deliver words of truth to people that they follow, resulting in change?	Yes	No
Do you prefer long-term relationship teaching to quick, spontaneous evangelism?	Yes	No
Do others consider you to be nurturing?	Yes	No
Do others consider you to be a good model of the Christian life?	Yes	No

Are you patient with the sin, immaturity, and need in others?	Yes	No
Are you protective of those God has entrusted you to disciple?	Yes	No
Do you see significant growth in those you disciple?	Yes	No
Do you enjoy preparing spiritual lessons and teachings for your disciples?	Yes	No
Are you lovingly tenacious when one of your disciples strays?	Yes	No

PROPHECY *(Romans 12:6; 1 Corinthians 12:28; Ephesians 4:11; Exodus 15:20; Judges 4:4; 2 Kings 22:14; Luke 2:3–38; Acts 2:9; Joel 2:28)*

Has God gifted you with strong verbal abilities when needed?	Yes	No
Are you often direct and to the point in conversations?	Yes	No
Do you inexplicably "sense" sin in those around you?	Yes	No
Are you often compelled to expose sins of specific people to them?	Yes	No
Do you find yourself to be bold when speaking from the Word of God?	Yes	No
Do you feel God's leadership when you speak to groups of people?	Yes	No
Are you sometimes controversial and misunderstood in what you say about sin?	Yes	No
Are you interested in politics, church issues, public concerns, or world issues?	Yes	No

Are messages you deliver to others relevant to them?	Yes	No
Do you tend to be uncompromising when God has given you a message to share?	Yes	No

TEACHING *(Romans 12:9; 1 Corinthians 12:28; Ephesians 4:11; 1 Peter 4:11; Matthew 28:19, 20; Colossians 1:28; Titus 2:3; 2 Timothy 1:5; Acts 18:24–26)*

Do you love studying God's Word deeply, using various tools?	Yes	No
Do you find yourself able to communicate clearly what you've studied?	Yes	No
Are you disciplined about completing study work, homework for classes you teach?	Yes	No
Do others whom you respect affirm that your teaching is accurate?	Yes	No
Are you comfortable disagreeing with people if what they teach is not accurate?	Yes	No
Do others consider you to be level-headed?	Yes	No
Do others consider you to be a model of Christian living?	Yes	No
Do those you teach suddenly understand something new when you share?	Yes	No

WISDOM *(1 Corinthians 12:8; Proverbs 2; 1 Kings 4:30–34; Luke 11:31)*

Do you enjoy solving problems that arise, especially among the body of believers?	Yes	No
Do you immediately begin to pray and seek God when problems arise?	Yes	No

Do you sense when people have conflict or problems even if not told?	Yes	No
Do others tend to seek you out to solve problems?	Yes	No
Are you comfortable delivering difficult truths to those in trouble?	Yes	No
Do you tend to have a lot of "common sense"?	Yes	No
Are you able to make God's Word practical to those around you?	Yes	No
Can you "sense" who is speaking truth when two parties are disagreeing?	Yes	No
Do you feel like God tells you how to present His Word?	Yes	No
Do others consider you to be insightful?	Yes	No

KNOWLEDGE *(1 Corinthians 12:8; Psalm 119:66; Proverbs 1:7; Proverbs 24:5; Ecclesiastes 1:16, 7:12; Romans 15:14; 1 Corinthians 8:1)*

Do you enjoy studying God's Word in a deeper way than others around you?	Yes	No
Do you enjoy accumulating biblical information, stats on believers, etc.?	Yes	No
Would you rather be alone to study than study with others?	Yes	No
Is solving a problem through research and study fun for you?	Yes	No
Do you prefer to observe a group discussion rather than enter into it right away?	Yes	No
Are you analytical?	Yes	No

Do you like to ask questions, especially about God's Word?	Yes	No
When you think you've learned something new in God's Word, do others confirm that it is accurate?	Yes	No
Do others clearly understand God's Word when you present it?	Yes	No
Are you agitated when others do not study God's Word before they share an opinion about it?	Yes	No

FAITH *(1 Corinthians 12:9; 1 Corinthians 13:13; Luke 8:42–48; Luke 8:48; Esther 4:16)*

Do you tend to be optimistic about what God will do in your life?	Yes	No
Are you often the last one still praying for something?	Yes	No
Do you have a childlike trust in God's ability to take care of you?	Yes	No
Do you tend to pray easily and perhaps more than others around you?	Yes	No
Do you often believe God for things that are impossible?	Yes	No
Would others consider you a visionary?	Yes	No
Are others inspired to believe by your faith?	Yes	No
Do you tend to have firm conviction that God will do what He says He will do in the Bible and expect New Testament power to be alive today?	Yes	No

HEALING *(1 Corinthians 12:9, 28–30; Matthew 4:23; Matthew 10:1; Matthew 17:6; Revelation 22:2)*

Have you seen people miraculously healed?	Yes	No
Have you laid hands on people and prayed for them, and seen them healed emotionally or physically?	Yes	No
Does God sometimes give you advice to deliver to those who are ill?	Yes	No
Do you feel overwhelming compassion for those who are sick?	Yes	No
Do you tend to be one of the last people believing that God can heal someone?	Yes	No
Are you comfortable being with severely ill people?	Yes	No
Is much of your prayer time used up to intercede for those who are ill?	Yes	No
Do you often feel led to pray for someone whom you "sense" is ill?	Yes	No

DISCERNMENT *(1 Corinthians 12:10; Matthew 7:22; Matthew 8:31; Matthew 10:8)*

Do you feel like you have a high dose of "women's intuition"?	Yes	No
Do you often feel inexplicably led to pray out of a sense of urgency?	Yes	No
Do you easily pick up on people who are not being truthful?	Yes	No
Can you often feel the presence of God's Spirit in a very real way?	Yes	No

Can you sometimes feel the
presence of evil in a very
real way?   Yes   No

When you pray for people, are
they sometimes delivered of
depression, sadness, physical
pain, or grief?   Yes   No

§ 2 • **Now that you've selected your top
three, write them here.**

    1. _____

    2. _____

    3. _____

Go back to the inventory and use the
Scriptures listed beside the three gifts you've
listed to simply explore each one. Meditate on
each verse and record any insights above by
the corresponding gift. The first few passages
are simply Scriptures that list this as a
common spiritual gift. Other verses contain
encouragement to use that gift or advice on how
to use it. Still others offer examples of someone
who used that gift as recorded in Scripture.

This has been a very powerful exercise for
me. As I have recorded what God teaches in
Scripture about my specific spiritual gifts, my
passion for them has grown, as has my
confidence. Most importantly, I've stayed
reliant on Him as the source of my gifts.

Remaining Gifts

There are a handful
of other gifts in
Scripture that are
important to
understand and be
aware of. They include
the following:

*Apostles (1 Corinthians
12:28)*

*Speaking in Tongues
(1 Corinthians 12:10)*

*Interpreting Tongues
(1 Corinthians 12:10)*

*Miraculous Powers
(1 Corinthians 12:10)*

*Celibacy
(1 Corinthians 7:7)*

*Voluntary Poverty
(1 Corinthians 13:3)*

*Martyrdom (1
Corinthians 13:3)*

*Hospitality
(1 Peter 4:9–10)*

*Missionary
(Eph. 3:6–9)*

What is the most important thing God has revealed to you today about your supernatural ability?

_____

_____

_____

_____

_____

MAKING IT WORK / MEDITATION

But to each one of us grace has been given as Christ apportioned it.
This is why it says: "When he ascended on high, he led captives
in his train and gave gifts to men."
—EPHESIANS 4:7–8

THE ADORNMENT OF CHARIS

What's My Supernatural Ability?

The second part of the Adornment of *Charis* is a specific, Spirit-given spiritual gift. I'd like you to meditate on the gift(s) God has prompted you to pursue. Specifically, I'd like you to ask Him what you are supposed to do with this gift. Where should you use it? How are you supposed to pursue understanding it?

Your meditation is Ephesians 4:7–8. I'd like you to meditate on this in conjunction with the three major gifts you've just selected to discuss with God in the coming weeks, months and years. Today is only the beginning of your answer to the question, "What is my supernatural ability?"

Now, turn to page 54 and fill in the second section under "Adornment of Charis."

GUIDED MEDITATION SESSION 10
Read Along in Five Little Questions: Chapter 15

QUESTION #4: AM I ENJOYING GOD?

You have made known to me the path of life; you will fill me with joy in your presence, with eternal pleasures at your right hand.
—Psalm 16:11

> "*Aim at heaven and you will get earth thrown in. Aim at earth and you will get neither.*"
> —C.S. Lewis

You're doing great! Keep it up. We're creating a map to guide you to the life God designed for you. Let's review.

Using the unlabeled diagram, label the two parts of the mark that we've now explored.

What are the questions that correspond to the following parts of the mark?

RING OF GRACE

Do _____ Need a _____ _____ of _____?

ADORNMENT OF CHARIS

Am I _____ Within My _____ _____?

What's My _____ _____?

The third part of the mark is the core of the bull's-eye. It's the most important part. If surrendering to Christ gets you into the Ring of Grace, these next two questions keep you there. Welcome to the "heart of the mark!"

Today I walked around my neighborhood like a crazy woman. I had my labradoodle and my iPod, everything I needed for a refreshing walk. The sun was brilliant. The snow still covered the ground with a blanket of white but was beginning to melt at a rapid pace that sent tiny bubbling streams through the neighborhood. Just as I rounded a corner, my new favorite Chris Tomlin song began bursting through my iPod. I couldn't help myself. It was all too much pleasure at once. I raised my hands and belted out words of worship at the top of my lungs.

I confess. This happens often. There are moments when on my morning walk with Stormie the sun is just right, the mountain foliage is at its peak or I hear the children playing in the neighborhood and I just sing to my Father . . . though I can't hold a tune!

I think God expects this sort of insanity from us. He beckons us to show off for Him as much as He does for us when He lights the stars each night. He urges us to chase after Him as shamelessly as He chases after us. If for no other reason, we should do this because there is nothing else that can satisfy so very much. And He wants us to enjoy Him. The first question as we look at the heart of the mark is, "Am I Enjoying God?"

Fill in the blanks for Psalm 16:11.

You have _____ _____ to me the _____ ___ _____; you will fill me with ____ in your presence, with _____ _____ at your right hand.

Living in the life plan God has designed brings joy and eternal pleasure. Living in our own life plan brings devastation. Our pleasure must be rooted in God or it will never last. And when our reservoir of joy runs dry, we'll find ourselves turning to lesser gods for a fix. And they will leave us woefully empty. That's what happened to a woman Jesus met at a well.

Maybe you know a woman who has had five husbands. I can't say that I do. But I do know a few who have been through divorce. Excruciating emotional pain, long nights of regrets, and years of rebuilding trust in people are some of the results I've seen. Imagine facing that alienation and rejection five times. That's what we find in the woman at the well. I can only imagine that she'd probably lost hope.

- Read John 4:7–29. After Jesus asks her to draw her water, what does He tell the woman at the well to do?

_____

_____

_____

_____

It was no small thing that Jesus spoke to this woman. Her sin was her bane of existence. No respectable man would speak to her. Jesus does. And, He goes right to the heart of the issue. Others would have gladly talked about the weather with her, avoiding the obvious. He doesn't. He talks about the great sin in her life. Jesus is like that. He goes straight to what ails us. Why?

- Read John 3:20. What does it tell us about sin?

_____

_____

_____

_____

Concealed sin keeps us from seeing the light of Christ . . . from enjoying God's glory and being moved to reflect it. You can't glorify God and allow sin to be concealed, buried, and hidden within you . . . no matter how old it might be. The woman at the well needed a fresh infusion of grace.

- Read John 4:28–29. With what attitude do you believe that this woman told the townspeople about Christ?

_____

_____

_____

_____

I think she was silly with enthusiasm. I think she couldn't contain her giggles.

Last year I was in Peru on a mission trip. An elderly woman approached two of the teenage girls on our trip and asked them to pray for her because she was sick. When they did, she began convulsing. The girls were scared, but urged on by their interpreters, they kept praying. The woman eventually stopped at which time they were able to share with her the truth of Jesus Christ. She wanted to surrender her life to

Christ. They prayed once again and this time when she was finished, she ran up to the bus the other team members were in and exuberantly thanked them in Spanish. She ran around through her little village smiling, rejoicing and jabbering happily. I believe she was enjoying God! I think the experience of the woman at the well was a lot like that—a great expression of joy.

• Read John 4:19–24. Once the sin is in the open, what do Jesus and the sinner woman discuss?

_____

_____

_____

_____

Who changes the subject?

_____

Of what significance can this drastic shift in conversation represent?

_____

_____

_____

_____

Once sin is out in the open, the woman uncomfortably shifts the conversation to a great debate of the day—where to worship. Though it was her smoke screen, I think there's something powerful in it for us.

The Samaritan woman asks Jesus if she should worship where her forefathers did or where the Jews worship. He says neither one. Funny thing, we're still constantly asking that question these days. We fight over whether there should be drums on stage, whether we should sing hymns, or whether worship can have instruments at all. He couldn't care less about who and where and with what. It's the heart that matters to Him. He wants us to worship abandoned in spirit and truth. No shows. No routine sense of obligation, but a total saturation of overwhelming gratitude for what He has done for us. Jesus Himself said, "Yet a time is coming and has now come when the true worshipers will worship the Father in spirit and truth, for they are the kind of worshipers that the Father seeks. God is a spirit, and His worshipers must worship in spirit and in truth" (John 4:23–24).

And so this sinful, five-times-divorced woman does worship! She cannot contain herself. No matter whom she might have been before, her spirit and countenance have changed. She has been in the very presence of God. She cannot help but praise Him. She invites the whole town to do the same.

And they do.

She is the first infused with His grace, *then* she enjoys Him. Out of that flows her usefulness! Though we don't know what her gifts were, I can only imagine that it went entirely against the grain of culture of that day for a five-times-divorced woman to publicly proclaim God's goodness. She must have been Spirit-filled with a gift of evangelism.

I see this pattern again and again. In 2006, I released a book entitled *The Secret of the Lord* which is primarily about confession and how the intimacy of the body of Christ can be, in fact, increased by it. It's so natural for us to feel that we will be alienated and unaccepted if our sins are known, but it rarely plays out that way. And where it does, I find the Spirit of the Lord is not at work.

One woman who read the book and who applied its truths wrote to me to share an exciting story. For years she'd been in a marriage where she kept a secret from her husband. Upon reading the book, she could contain it no longer and finally decided to share her shameful past with Him. Expecting rejection, she found God's forgiveness in His arms. She received a fresh infusion of God's grace through her husband's forgiveness. Almost immediately, a deep passion of hers that had died years ago was rekindled. When she was younger, she had wanted to be a missionary in China. After a few weeks, she had to share this good secret with her husband as well. Within six months, he had her on a short-term mission trip to China. No slow boat when God is involved!

Get infused with His grace and this task of enjoying God will just burst out of you. And, he'll put your spiritual gifts to work like never before. I promise. Enjoying God is not something we do out of duty, or routine, or dead works. It is a spontaneous response of being in His presence and being so overwhelmed by the beauty of that place that we can't help but speak of it with every breath.

This joy explodes within us, giving us the courage to move forth with the unique gifts God has entrusted to us.

In both stories—the woman at the well and my friend who went to China—what prompted their joy?

_____

_____

_____

_____

_____

I think it was knowledge of God's grace that ultimately infused it. And I personally have never enjoyed God more than in the moments that I've been aware of both my sin and His grace in a deep way. But, hopefully you and I have either matured or are maturing past hiding deep sin. So, how do we enjoy God on a daily basis? The Bible speaks of many sources of joy in God. Let's look at just two books or we might be here until tomorrow!

Each of the verses below speaks of one specific thing that God *does* for us, prompting us to enjoy Him.

Psalm 5:11
Psalm 20:5
Psalm 94:19

We are protected by our God. We are made victorious over evil. And we are consoled by Him. These things bring joy. I've noticed that people who give God credit for even the small things in their lives tend to be happier and more at peace. So, even though I'm kind of a quiet girl, I've adopted the habit of praising Him out loud when I hear good news.

Each of the verses below speaks of one specific thing that God *gives* to us, prompting us to enjoy Him.

Psalm 65:8, 13; 16:12; 98:8
Psalm 98:6; 126:2
Proverbs 12:20; 23:24; 15:20

The beauty of nature. The emotional swell of music in our hearts. Our children. These things are given to us to promote a sense of enjoying God. A walk with my faithful friend, Stormie, always sparks a sense of enjoying God, especially on those days when the sun shines particularly beautifully, I'm blessed to catch a sunset or the mountains are in full fall foliage. Sometimes, I just raise my hands and sing as I walk. (Especially if it is dark and I'm certain no one will notice. Do you think any of the neighbors find me strange?)

§ From the suggestions above, other Scriptures stored in your heart and life experiences, what prompts a sense of enjoying God in your life?

_____

_____

_____

_____

_____

Is there something you can do to experience this more often?

_____

_____

_____

_____

_____

MAKING IT WORK  MEDITATION

You have made known to me the path of life; you will fill me with joy in your presence, with eternal pleasures at your right hand.
—PSALM 16:11

THE HEART OF THE MARK
Am I Enjoying God?

Are you enjoying God? If you're fully infused with His grace and pursuing your unique spiritual gifts in an environment that's right for your behavioral strengths, you'll be more likely to find joy. But ultimately, it is found in just being with Him.

When was the last time you spent one hour just being with Him? Want to rock your world? Schedule an hour to be alone with God before you move to the next session. Schedule this to include whatever fills you up and causes you to enjoy God. You'll feel His presence. I promise. As you meditate on Psalm 16:11 and the truth of it revealed through the Samaritan woman's experience, ask yourself if you are enjoying God. Ask Him to show you what you need to do to find pleasure in Him.

Your meditation assignment is Psalm 16:11.

Now, turn to page 55 and fill in the first section under "The Heart of the Mask."

GUIDED MEDITATION SESSION 11
Read Along In Five Little Questions: Chapter 16

QUESTION #5: AM I GLORIOUS?

*So whether you eat or drink or whatever you do,
do it all for the glory of God.*
—1 Corinthians 10:31

> " *What we are is God's gift to us, what we
> become is our gift to God.*
> —Eleanor Powell, 1940s actress and tap dancer "

Congratulations! You're ready to answer the last of the *Five Little Questions*. Now, let's review where we've been. Remember I don't do this to bore you, but because when you're in the life God designed for you, you must stay vigilant. You must constantly reevaluate by asking yourself the Five Little Questions.

Using the diagram, label all three parts of the mark.
What are the questions you've learned so far?
Ring of Grace
1.

Adornment of Charis
2.
3.

Heart of the Mark
4.

Imagine you're the mayor of a city of two million families. Now, imagine you've been called to a meeting with your boss to discuss your job. He wants to get you away from it all, so he takes you up into the mountains. Now imagine your boss is kind of like Charlie from *Charlie's Angels*. Never shows His face. But this time will be different. What you see whacks you out so much that your hair stands on end for days and everyone wonders what in the world happened to you.

Moses didn't have to imagine. It really happened to him. And God was that boss.

Read Exodus 33:12–23. What is Moses' state of mind?

_____

_____

_____

_____

_____

Moses seems as stressed out as I would be if I were running an operation to house, feed, clothe, and employee a city of that size. He bemoans a bit when he says, "You have been telling me, 'Lead these people,' but you have not let me know whom you will send with me." He's feeling understaffed.

Do I know what that feels like. My husband and I operate three ministries, two of which have national impact—one here in the U.S. and one in Zambia. There are never enough people on the team. Never. Of course, it was kind of like that when I was primarily a stay-at-home mom too.

What I'm saying is this. Sounds like a typical rat race moment for Moses. He felt he was working hard and getting nowhere.

What does God promise in verse 14?

_____

_____

_____

_____

Rest. He promises He will give us rest. Is that what you get when you are serving God? Is it filling you up because you are infused with His grace, working in accordance to how he's created and gifted you and enjoying Him? If not, something's not right.

FROM FIVE LITTLE QUESTIONS...

Sadly the heard of the mark is where we get all messed up, which brings us back to where we began. We think glorifying God means we're supposed to jump into the rate race of

Christian works, supposed to say yes to every request the church makes of us, supposed to be busy, busy, busy . . . but nothing could be a greater deception.

What we have all too often today is rat-race Christians doing, doing, doing and never sitting in the presence of God.

To glorify God, we must first rest in Him.

I'm in a crunch zone right now. I'm burning the midnight oil to get this manuscript to my editor tonight. At the same time, I'm petitioning federal leaders because my family—Bob, Robby, Lexi, and I—are completely in love with a precious thirteen-year-old orphan who lives in China and we need to expedite some government paperwork or we will miss a deadline to get her out of the nation before she is fourteen. My husband is traveling. And—this one is big—Robby is DRIVING! Twelve years ago, this kind of week would have pushed me over the edge . . . especially if it came at that emotionally wealthy time of the month.

But, I would have to say that I feel protected and rested. Living in the life God designed for me —which regularly includes one hour of prayer time each morning, even today when I didn't feel I could spare a moment to breathe—is one of rest regardless of the pace. I'm not saying I'm not occasionally physically exhausted, but I rarely get emotionally and spiritually depleted anymore.

And when I do find myself exhausted, I have to go back to the questions and ask myself what needs to be adjusted.

Do I need a fresh infusion of grace?

Am I working in agreement with my created personality?

What is my supernatural ability?

Am I enjoying God?

Am I glorious?

Am I glorious? Are you?

What does Moses ask for in Exodus 33:18?

_____

_____

_____

_____

_____

How does God respond in verses 19–23?

_____

_____

_____

_____

Moses wanted to see the brilliance of God. He, like you and I, craved a look that truly revealed His intimate friend and Sovereign One. More than he was understaffed, he was insecure. He wanted a deeper taste of God experientially.

God could not show Himself to Moses. I personally think it would have singed the poor guy to the core had he seen our God. And yet, He lovingly takes Moses' hand, covers Moses oh-so-protectively, and allows His servant to see Him when He has passed. Moses gets to see God's back.

Meditate for a moment and consider what this could mean? What parallel to our lives today could be seen in only being able to see God's back?

_____

_____

Seeing God from behind means that we can only see where He has already been. We can fathom His glory only thorough what He has already done and where He has moved.

Last year, my husband and I took twenty-nine people with us to our ministry headquarters in Zambia. Headquarters is a lofty term. Very lofty. We were in the middle of African grass sleeping in modest structures. As we attempted to sleep on our first night, Bob was snoring like I've never heard. I kept trying to gently reach out from under the mosquito net on my little cot to nudge him, but no matter how I moved him he would not stop. Finally, I just woke him and praise God I did. His nose was bleeding like Old Faithful. Honestly, I did not know if I loved him or my single roll of toilet paper more when I saw him head for it!

An hour passed and we could not stop the bleeding. Each time we replaced a soaked rag, his nose gushed. After a few hours of not sleeping, we packed his nose and lay there fairly comatose.

Wild thoughts run through your head when you've just been on a plane for twenty-two hours and you're lying next to your husband in a Third World nation as he bleeds profusely. I was very fearful. I didn't want to be, but I really felt I needed God to show up. I wanted to see Him. I needed His glory that night. I prayed through most of it, sleeping very little.

When we unpacked Bob's nose in the morning, it all started back up again.

Now, I'd been to a few of the local "hospitals" and I wouldn't want my dog treated there. We'd been warned to be careful about medical care, but we didn't know what to do. So, I gathered Bob's passport and medical records and asked one of our Zambian friends to take him to the hospital while I tended to our team. Just as they were going to get in the car, one of the team members came out of his room.

"I heard Bob has a bloody nose," said James. "I had one a week or so ago and had to go to the hospital. My doctor sent me here with a few cauterization kits in case it happened while I was here. Would you like one?"

He passed me in the night. I'm fairly certain He placed His great protective hand over that little African cottage. I didn't see His face, but He was there.

It made me radiant!

I walked around all day just silly with praise for my God. Before I got on that plane in Washington, D.C., He saw to it that it had a nose cauterization kit for my husband. What a God. Every detail of my life is in His care.

On that day, I was glorious.

Read Exodus 34:29–35. What does it say about Moses?

_____

_____

_____

_____

_____

_____

Moses' face was so radiant that it frightened the people when they saw him. Frightened or not, the people could clearly see God in Moses. Moses didn't get the ability to glorify God down with the masses while he was doing things for God. He got the ability to glorify God from being with Him.

Be with Him.

You'll be glorious.

MAKING IT WORK  MEDITATION

So whether you eat or drink or whatever you do,
do it all for the glory of God.
—1 CORINTHIANS 10:31

THE HEART OF THE MARK
Am I Glorious?

Did you spend an hour with God as I suggested in the last chapter? If not, let me invite you again to give it a try. If you did, don't you want more of it? You can only say, "Look at me" with confidence if your life is hidden in the presence of God. Won't you step out of the rat race to sit with Him today?

As you meditate today, consider the question, "Am I Glorious?"

Your meditation assignment is 1 Corinthians 10:31.

_____

_____

_____

_____

_____

_____

_____

_____

Now, turn to page 55 and fill in the second section under "The Heart of the Mask."

GUIDED MEDITATION SESSION 12

Read Along in Five Little Questions: Chapters 17 & 18

STEPPING INTO A GOD-DESIGNED LIFE

Then birds of prey came down on the carcasses,
but Abram drove them away.
—Genesis 15:11

> " *The credit belongs to the man who is actually in the arena . . . who at the best knows in the end the triumph of achievement; and who at worst, if he fails, at least fails while daring greatly, so that his place shall ever be with those cold timid souls who neither know victory nor defeat.*
> —Teddy Roosevelt "

A few years ago, I was stuffed into an eighteen-passenger van late on a Saturday night with my team members. We were on our way home from the Washington, D.C., area where we'd just completed an amazing weekend of ministry with about four hundred teens, many of whom surrendered to Christ for the first time or made commitments to be freshly infused with God's grace. We were euphoric as we drove until suddenly a great clunking sound jolted us.

The van was full of pastors and ministers. Translation: No one knew how to fix it! But we got on the phone with a guy who did. He had us look around and tell him what we saw. After being stranded there for about thirty minutes, the news wasn't good. We needed a part that would be difficult to find late on a Saturday night, and it would take about two hours to repair once we had the part.

I don't know what came over me. . . . well, yes I do. The Holy Spirit will sometimes call you to do embarrassing things! With all the authority my blond head could muster, I said, "We need to lay hands on this van and pray for God to fix it."

The guys on the team looked at me as if my blond locks were natural and I had the brains to go with them! I lost a bit of my confidence then.

Until my friend Suzy stepped up to the van, placed her hand on its big white hood and bowed her head. I did likewise. I guess the others were beginning to understand that I was serious. They bowed their heads, too, and then I just asked.

"Lord, we love you," I began. "We've served you well this weekend. I know you want us to be home with our families and you want the pastors in this van to be in their churches to minister in the morning. Will you please fix this van?"

We piled into the van silently.

Jonathan turned the van on.

We drove home.

We were victorious, but the evening reminded me that the enemy is always at work to diminish our joy and passion to pursue the life God has designed for us. He often sends his "birds of prey" to gnaw at our sacrifice.

FROM FIVE LITTLE QUESTIONS...

Knowing that they're coming is half the battle. I mean, it'd be great if I could just tell you life will be peachy now that you're living in the life God designed for you, but it won't be.

What do you do? God victoriously records for our encouragement what He saw Abraham do. "But Abram drove them away!"

I think it takes great courage to live a life that is designed by God. I wouldn't dare do it alone. My friends, like Suzy, stand beside me and give me courage.

- Read 3 John. It is a short letter. Who is it written to?

_____

_____

_____

Who is writing it?

_____

_____

In verses, 1, 2, 5 and 11, how does John address Gaius?

This letter is such a source of comfort. Gaius is attempting to live in the life God has designed for him. John writes to encourage him in his Christian life. Oh, that our e-mails would ring with the same flavor of passion and pride for our Christian friends. Wouldn't it strengthen your heart to receive a letter like this?

We need friends to do this intentionally for us. And we need to do it for them.

List five people who stand beside you and help you live a godly life?

1.

2.

3.

4.

5.

Which one of them is either doing this study with you or easily accessible to you and could help you pray through your pursuit of the life God designed for the next six months? (This person will review your life M.A.P. with you, sign it, pray every day, and stay in contact with you for accountability.)

Having determined who that person will be, what goals does God want you to pursue?

_____

_____

_____

_____

Take a lengthy period of time to meditate and pray about your life M.A.P. today.

MAKING IT WORK  MEDITATION

> *Then birds of prey came down on the carcasses,*
> *but Abram drove them away.*
> —GENESIS 15:11

Today, I want you to turn to your M.A.P. as you focus on Genesis 15:11. Ask yourself what adjustments need to be made in your life to live the life God has designed for you. Rekindle any dreams God has allowed to surface or resurface as you do this study. Ponder your next step of action and be poised to fight off any birds of prey that flutter around to discourage you.

Upon completion of journaling, turn back to your map to review it and sign it with your accountability partner.

Turn to page 55. Note that there are places for you and an accountability partner to sign your M.A.P. If you're doing this as a small group, sign this today. If not, consider who can help you with accountability.

LEADER'S APPENDIX

There is power in numbers!

If you are doing this as a group, thank you. I believe this book has the greatest chance to work if accountability is available to my dear friends who read it. I like to keep it simple. You have twelve weeks of study material. You can opt to read along in the main book if you'd like. I strongly encourage that for a fuller view of the material.

As you come together each week, simply:

§ Share the answer to each chapter's key question which has this symbol . . . § . . . beside it.

Encourage women to read their journaling to one another. Don't force this, but it's a great way to open them up and help them to achieve intimacy.

As you get to the M.A.P., review one another's answers. Give each person time to share and be prayed over. Take your time. Huddle around each woman and touch her as you pray for her.

Keep it simple.

At the end of the study, pair women up to be accountability and prayer partners for the next six months as encouraged in the last session.

You always can watch my Web site at dannahgresh.com to see if we have any new resources to support you with this or other studies I've prepared for women.

NOTES

SESSION 2

1. John Piper, *Desiring God* (Sisters, Oregon: Multnomah), 2003

SESSION 3

1. Beth Moore, verbally quoted in DVD teaching of "The Beloved Disciple" (Nashville, Lifeway)

SESSION 4

1. Brennan Manning, *The Rabbi's Heartbeat* (Colorado Springs: NavPress, 2007), 24.

SESSION 6

1. Philip Yancey, *Rumors of Another World* (Grand Rapids, Michigan; Zondervan, 2003), 144.

SESSION 8

1. Charles F. Boyd, *Different Children, Different Needs* (Sisters, Oregon: Multnomah, 1994), 27.

SESSION 9

1. Barna Research Online, "Awareness of Spiritual Gifts Is Changing," http://www.barna.org/FlexPage.aspx?Page=BarnaUpdate&Barna UpdateID=81 (February 5, 2001).

2. Rebecca St. James, "Cool Conversations/Interviews," http://www.thesource4ym.com/interviews/rsjames.asp (October 3, 2000).